SPEEDWAY

IN THE SOUTH-WEST

SPEEDWAY

IN THE SOUTH-WEST

Tony Lethbridge

TEMPUS

First published 2003

PUBLISHED IN THE UNITED KINGDOM BY:
Tempus Publishing Ltd
The Mill, Brimscombe Port
Stroud, Gloucestershire GL5 2QG

PUBLISHED IN THE UNITED STATES OF AMERICA BY:
Tempus Publishing Inc.
2 Cumberland Street
Charleston, SC 29401

British Library Cataloguing in Publication Data.
A catalogue record for this book is available from the British Library.

ISBN 0 7524 2915 9

Typesetting and origination by Tempus Publishing.
Printed in Great Britain by Midway Colour Print, Wiltshire

CONTENTS

INTRODUCTION

The South-West is not exactly an epicentre of sporting prowess, but a mention of speedway invariably prompts the comment 'Oh, I used to go to that.' If you happen to be in Exeter the reply will also include the name of Ivan Mauger or Cyril Roger, in Poole it will be Ken Middleditch or Malcolm Simmons. My good friend Gordon Day once suggested that no matter what door you knocked on in Poole at least one person in that household will have attended a Pirates match. For almost 75 years the South-West tracks have been attracting both locals and holiday makers along to witness the thrills and spills of speedway. Some have been more successful than others in this respect, to which the following pages will testify.

Speedway has certainly played an important role in the lives of many West Country folk and the current wealth of literature detailing the sport's colourful history proves just how much interest speedway generates. In many ways it is a nostalgia thing. Regular enthusiasts recall their early heroes with wonder, even if the records show that they didn't quite score as many points as you always thought they did. Notable milestones in life are forever associated with memorable matches, events and even crashes. For speedway is about people. Although the object of this volume is to outline the history of the various South-West tracks, it must be remembered that none of this would have happened had it not been for the larger-than-life characters who make it tick.

First there are the promoters, beginning with the autocratic Leonard Glanfield who opened Exeter in 1929, Bill Dutton who ran the Falcons in the fifties and later opened Weymouth, the long-serving Knot family at Poole, super showman Trevor Redmond at St Austell who would run the car park and sell programmes before changing into his leathers in time for the first race. Thirty years later, TR's style rubbed off on Brian Annear, who would roar around the wonderful Clay Country Moto Parc on his monkey bike in baggy shorts and T-shirt while visiting promoters wore the regulation blazer and flannels. Then there was millionaire business man Mervyn Stewkesbury, desperately trying to bring success to Weymouth before eventually finding it at Poole. Matt Ford and Mike Golding who at the millennium made the Pirates the best-supported team in Britain. Flamboyant Bernard Curtiss lasted but a single season at Plymouth while stylish Wally Mawdsley launched his multi-track empire at Exeter and after twenty years was replaced first by Fleet Street journalist Peter Oakes and later by shy, quiet Colin Hill.

Then, of course, there are the riders. The superstars, Ivan Mauger, Tony Rickardsson, Jason Crump, Mark Loram, Malcolm Simmons, Simon Wigg; the big-time favourites, Ken Middleditch, Jack Geran, Tony Lewis, Scott Autrey, Martin Yeates, Neil Street, Bruce

Cribb, Goog Hoskin, Odd Fossengen, Steve Schofield. And, of course, the tearaways; Broncho Slade, Vaclav Verner, Chris Julian, Chris Blewett, Richard Green and many, many more. Everyone has their own special favourites and to cram in all their exploits was just not possible. I hope that the following pages give a taste of the glories that have been 'Speedway in the South West' over the past seventy-five years.

ACKNOWLEDGEMENTS

To attempt to plot the history of one track let alone half-a-dozen would be impossible without the generous help and advice of several like-minded friends. Before I record their contribution to this book, I should also point out that it is equally impossible to record every detail relating to the teams and clubs chronicled within these pages. Exeter and Poole alone have between them raced some 110 seasons, and the official history of the Falcons has so far reached three volumes and is still growing. Therefore, I must emphasise this is an overview of the West Country tracks covering 74 years.

My sincere thanks go to everyone who has helped complete what has proved to be a much tougher task than I expected. That doyen of speedway historians, Glynn Shailes, has been a source of encouragement, help and advice throughout and his wealth of knowledge has never been more gratefully received.

My thanks also go to Graham Hambly, Gordon Day, Dave Stallworthy, Robin Playsted, Bob Radford, Peter Oakes, Fred Paul, Eric Abbot, John Yeo, Mick Barnes and Ian Williams, who have all provided vital information, while, as usual, Rob Doran has allowed me unlimited access to his photo archives.

I would also like to acknowledge that my research was greatly aided by being able to draw on the invaluable information provided by *Speedway Star*, *Speedway World* and *Speedway Post*, as well as the excellent *Speedway Researcher*, in particular the pre-war league tables compiled by Mike Terran, and Peter Morrish's excellent book, *British Speedway Leagues 1946-1964*. My thanks also go to Norman Jacobs for suggesting that I undertake the task in the first place. Last, but by no means least, I'd like to thank my wife, Christine, for her encouragement, constructive criticism and total support.

Tony Lethbridge

PART I

EXETER, ALPHINGTON AND HALDON

EXETER

The first speedway meeting to be staged in the South West took place at Exeter's County Ground stadium on Saturday 9 March 1929. The new sport was brought to the city by locally born Leonard Glanfield who had been employed by A.J. Hunting, one of the men responsible for introducing speedway to Britain the previous year, as an announcer at London White City. Glanfield quickly realised the advantages of running his own track. Remembering the County Ground from his youth, he soon agreed a lease with the Exeter (Rugby) Football Club for £300 a year. The steeply banked tarmac cycle track circling the rugby pitch was torn up and replaced with a 413-yard cinder circuit surrounded by a heavy wire and board safety fence, forty electric floodlights and a tannoy system. The new speedway track was constructed in just two months.

Great excitement surrounded the build-up to the opening meeting and Glanfield was not disappointed when 11,000 spectators including the Mayor and civic dignitaries arrived to see the new phenomenon for themselves. The impact was enormous.

'Thrilling, breathtaking, hair raising!' enthused one local newspaper. Les Dallimore won the first race and the Exeter Handicap final while second place man Ron Johnson was victorious in the Golden Helmet scratch event. Johnson quickly became the crowd's favourite along with 'Wizard' Frank Arthur who set the one lap record with a time of 20.6 seconds.

During 1929 meetings were held twice a week, on Wednesdays and Saturdays. Glanfield built on his successful start by booking the top stars of the day. Arthur and Johnson would remain the most popular attractions, but so too were Vic Huxley, 'Sprouts' Elder the tall American, Englishmen Roger Frogley and Tom Farndon, 'Cyclone' Billy Lamont and the fabled lady racer Fay Taylour. Exeter also had its own nucleus of riders based at the County Ground. These included several Australians – Noel Johnson, Jack Bishop, Bert Spencer and 'Hard Luck' Harold Stevens – along with South Africa's Les Barker, Richard 'Buggie' Fleeman (who had helped to build the track), and Frank 'Buster' Buckland, a local electrician and rugby player whose enthusiasm had been fired while installing the floodlighting.

The first Speedway Great Revel, a star-studded gala meeting, was staged at the County Ground on Tuesday 25 June, and proved to be one of the highlights of the 1929 season. It was probably the best-attended meeting in the track's 73-year history attracting a crowd of well over 16,000, with another 3,000 turned away. Frank Arthur won the *Express & Echo* Gold Cup, Ron Stokes the Pike's Silver Column, and 'Buggie' Fleeman the *Gazette* Gold Casket. Jack Bishop, who finished second to Arthur in the main event, received a silver cup donated by the Royal Naval College at Dartmouth for the fastest four laps.

The second Speedway Revel on 30 July attracted a crowd of only 11,000, but they were treated to another all-star programme. Exeter's Jack Bishop beat Billy Lamont to

An aerial view of the County Ground stadium.

win the main event, the Chevrolet Gold Cup. The line-up for the meeting also included Gus Kuhn, Roger Frogley and Max Grosskreutz as well as the local favourites.

August saw Exeter's Australian riders achieve a notable success when they went to London and beat Stamford Bridge 13-8 in a team match. Until that night the Pensioners remained unbeaten, having won twelve of their thirteen Southern League matches.

A third Revel was staged in early September. Due to the late withdrawal, through injury, of several top stars it was left to the local riders to provide the thrills. Jack Bishop, now billed as the Exeter champion, won the Hospital Cup while Lew Lancaster was victorious in the Exeter Handicap. The meeting also included a team match against Coventry, which Exeter won comfortably 17-4.

Until June crowds had been consistently good but as the summer progressed interest began to wane and attendances declined. News that Frank Arthur would not be riding due to injury had a dramatic effect on the attendance on 18 September. Prior to the meeting the management distributed leaflets outside the stadium explaining the situation and as a result only 4,000 people went through the turnstiles. This was 1,000 down on the previous Saturday's meeting and the smallest crowd since speedway started at Exeter. The future looked grim but hopes of reviving the track's fortunes lay with the Fourth Revel to be held a week later. Sadly although 12,000 people watched the meeting Glanfield's difficulties continued. Frank Arthur was still unfit so was replaced by Geoff Taylor who, travelling down with fellow Aussie Max Grosskreutz, was stopped for speeding by the police and did not arrive at the track until 9 p.m. Harold Stevens, still nursing broken ribs from a recent crash at Southampton won the Chevrolet Cup while Billy Lamont won the All Star Scratch final from Vic Huxley. On this occasion Lamont rode Frank Arthur's famous Harley Davidson Peashooter machine. The various delays meant that the meeting did not finish until 10.40 p.m. Sadly the Revel did not trigger off the anticipated revival and the crowd at the following Saturday's meeting dropped below 3,000 despite an attractive programme, which included a ladies' race between Fay Taylour and Cornwall's Dorothy Bunt.

The following week's meeting was cancelled as Arthur was still unavailable, but he raced in what proved to be the last meeting to be staged by Leonard Glanfield's Southern Speedways company on Wednesday 9 October. The evening was marred by a serious accident in which Harold Stevens fell while chasing Arthur and was hit by Charlie Swift. Stevens was taken to hospital with a fractured thigh. Two days later came the announcement that speedway had been suspended. Glanfield's promoting licence was later suspended by the ACU, but official records show that his ban was lifted the following spring when all outstanding debts were cleared.

There was one final meeting, a charity event staged by the riders as part of the St Thomas carnival on Wednesday 16 October. Racing began at 9 p.m. at the conclusion of the carnival procession. Frank Arthur and Ray Tauser agreed to take part and helped to attract a 7,000 crowd. The takings were divided among the riders with Arthur generously donating his winnings to the cause.

Crystal Palace promoters Fred Mockford and Cecil Smith clearly saw the potential of Exeter and took over in 1930. The public welcomed them but the new promoters soon realised that they faced considerable opposition from a group of local residents who had taken out an injunction to prevent the speedway continuing.

The first meeting in April was delayed for 24 hours due to heavy rain. Ron Johnson topped the bill, and defeated his namesake Noel Johnson in a match race series. The new promotion made several improvements to the organisation and there was less delay between races. There was certainly no shortage of top riders. Jack Parker, Roger Frogley and Tom Farndon all appeared in the early meetings along with Danish stars Walter Ryle and Kai Anderson but Exeter lost team matches against Cardiff, Coventry and West Ham, who included Tiger Stevenson and Bluey Wilkinson.

Noel Johnson was brought in to strengthen the Exeter team and helped them beat Wembley 39-15 on 21 May for their first win of the season.

Ladies' races remained popular and in June Miss Sunny Somerset was defeated by Dorothy Bunt. Exeter gained a second team victory when they beat Crystal Palace, albeit aided by engine failures for Ron Johnson and Joe Francis.

The legal injunction finally went to court in July and Mockford and Smith won the day. They celebrated with an all-star Victory Meeting. The line-up included Ivor Creek, Shep Shepherd, Harry Taft, Wally Kilminster and Joe Francis but it was Exeter's Frank Buckland who came out on top in the Big Six Contest. Over the following weeks Buckland won several more major events before losing to Colin Watson at the end of August.

An unofficial test match between England and Australia, led by Bluey Wilkinson was won by the Colonials 28-24. Not quite so successful was the Exeter £200 Open Championship for which seven top riders failed to arrive, but which was won by Ron Johnson. Generally, despite continued opposition from the residents, the season was a success with attendances averaging between 8,000 and 9,000.

Confidence was high as Mockford and Smith embarked on their second season. The 1931 season opened on 14 May with a National Trophy match against High Beech. Lew Lancaster had now joined the Exeter team, which also included Buckland, Reg Beer, Jack Douglas, Bill Hamblin, and Clarrie Eldridge. Sadly they were no match for the Forresters who won both matches and went through 120-77.

The ever-popular Ron Johnson remained a regular visitor beating his Crystal Palace team mate Joe Francis in a match race series. They then competed against each other again in a Homeland *v.* Colonies match in June. The Homeland won 34-17 while Johnson scored more than half his team's total.

Exeter lost to Plymouth in the opening match at Pennycross but gained revenge by winning 33-20 in the return at the County Ground. Another crowd favourite, Frank Arthur, also appeared in June but along with Tom Farndon was beaten by Buckland. Lea Bridge beat Exeter in a team match in July but by now the public interest in speedway was again declining and the promotion were losing money. The final meeting, in which Lionel Van Praag and George Greenwood appeared, took place on 22 July and the promoting company, County Speedways, went into liquidation.

Exeter Motor Club staged a limited number of amateur meetings during 1934, which attracted crowds of 4,000, when Plymouth riders were allowed to compete in a class for professionals. But the ACU stepped in and banned professional riders, after which the amateur meetings were soon abandoned.

League racing was introduced for the first time when racing returned to the County Ground again in 1947. During the intervening war years the stadium had been taken over by the military as a camp for British, and then later American, troops. A new promoting company, Exeter Motor Sports Ltd, headed by Frank Buckland, quickly refurbished the track and the safety fence. The original 1929 fence, now in a decrepit state, was replaced using the only materials available, steel sheets from redundant Morrison indoor air-raid shelters. They are still in use although disliked by many visiting riders.

To aid the formation of a new National League Division III, 'Tiger' Stevenson ran a series of winter training schools to find the riders to fill the eight new teams of which Exeter would be one. The new era began on Monday 14 April, when a number of Stevenson's trainees competed in 'The Battle for Team Places' which was won by Charlie Hayden. All the races had to be started on the green light as the new electric starting gate was not delivered until the next day.

A week later the pick of the riders were invited back for a 'Possibles *v.* Probables' match. Top scorer for the winning Possibles was Cyril Roger with a 12-point maximum. The line-up for the Falcons opening match was Bernard 'Broncho' Slade, Les Trim, Cyril Roger, Allan Chambers, Ted Moore and Sid Hazzard, with Don Hardy and Tom Crutcher at reserve.

Promoters : COUNTY SPEEDWAYS Ltd.

EXETER TRACK — COUNTY GROUNDS.

Managing Director: **F. E. Mockford, M.I.M.T.**
Director   -   -   **Cecil L. Smith**

**Official
Programme
3d.**

OPENING MEETING

Wednesday, April 9th, 1930 at 7.45 p.m.

SPECIAL MATCH RACE

RON JOHNSON   *v*   **NOEL JOHNSON**
(Australia)   **(Exeter)**

INTERNATIONAL RACE

DENMARK   *v*   **EXETER**

A 1930 programme cover.

OFFICIAL PROGRAMME 6d.

EXETER
SPEEDWAY

MOTOR SPORTS (EXETER) LTD.
County Ground Sports Stadium, St. Thomas, Exeter.   Phone 5231

MONDAY, 5th JULY, 1948, at 7.30 p.m.

National League Match

EXETER v. HASTINGS

Fifteenth Meeting

N O   B E T T I N G   A L L O W E D

W. V. COLE & SONS, EXETER

A 1947 programme cover.

The 1947 Exeter Falcons. From left to right, back row: Tom Crutcher, Charlie Hayden, Ted Moore, Bill Williams. Front row: Allan Chambers, Les Trim, Broncho Slade, Don Hardy, Cyril Roger.

After losing 63-20 at Eastbourne in a challenge match, the Falcons recorded four wins against Eastbourne, Plymouth and Hanley and away at Plymouth. This set the pattern for the season: huge home victories due to the extra advantage of the big steeply banked County Ground track, and defeats on the more conventional flat away tracks, Plymouth being the one exception, which resulted in the Falcons finishing in mid-table. Exeter's only home defeat came at the hands of the newly crowned champions, Eastbourne, in the North *v.* South cup. Roger proved to be the find of the season and became virtually unbeatable around the County Ground.

Frank Buckland spent the winter in Australia and returned with three promising riders, Norman Clay, Hugh Geddes and Keith Gurtner. Cyril Roger's brother Bert joined him at the County ground for 1948, along with Arthur Pilgrim. A strong team plus exceptional home advantage ensured plenty of big wins for the Falcons, who now enjoyed considerable success on their travels. Local rivals Plymouth were the only side to take League points from the County Ground as the Falcons relentlessly headed towards the championship. Victory at Southampton followed by wins at Plymouth, Wombwell, Stoke and Poole ensured the Falcons won their first League title.

Cyril Roger was again virtually unstoppable at Exeter and his phenomenal success resulted in him being recalled to New Cross mid-way through the season, after which brother Bert went on to head the Falcons' scorers with a record 419 points from forty-three matches in his first year of League racing. The big home wins eventually affected the attendances to such an extent that Buckland threatened to move the team to a better-supported venue.

Exeter's hopes of being promoted to the Second Division were quickly dashed on the basis of the ground facilities and attendance figures, which did not meet SCB requirements. The Falcons suffered a further blow when both Bert Roger and Don Hardy were recalled by New Cross.

Arthur Pilgrim became skipper 1949 and Vic Gent was signed from Plymouth but although Don Hardy was eventually transferred from New Cross the Falcons failed to maintain their championship-winning form. Exeter beat Plymouth in the first round of the National Trophy but then lost to Stoke while an early injury to Norman Clay and the premature death of Stan Hodson from TB seriously hit their efforts to defend the title. Exeter eventually finished the season in seventh place after Bill Dutton had taken over as team manager. The year ended tragically when Norman Clay was killed in a track crash at Sydney Showground.

If the Falcons' fortunes had declined in 1949 they hit rock bottom in 1950. Two new Australians, Ken Walsh and Jack Bedkober, were signed while Ted Moore, who had seriously injured his knee in 1947, returned to join Hardy, Johnnie Myson, Hugh Geddes, Arthur Pilgrim and Vic Gent. In a bid to boost attendances, the management unwisely changed the race night from Monday to Friday.

The new riders took a while to settle and the Falcons struggled in most of their early fixtures. The exception was in the National Trophy where, having lost heavily at Leicester, Exeter fought back to draw on aggregate before winning away at Blackbird Road in the replay. Success was short-lived, however, as Oxford put the Falcons out in the next round.

Oxford also won at the County Ground in the National League leading to a run of home defeats. These coupled with the unpopular Friday race night saw attendances

Bob (left) and Cyril (right) Roger.

plummet. To add to Exeter's difficulties several riders sustained injuries. The financial position became so desperate that Hugh Geddes was sold to Swindon for £550. Bill Downton, his replacement, suffered serious head injuries after only three weeks in Exeter colours while Bob Wigg, signed from Plymouth, had an equally short County Ground career.

Towards the end of the season the management sensibly switched back to Mondays and the Falcons' results began to pick up. They eventually finished seventh out of ten.

The year 1951 saw a marked improvement in Exeter's fortunes. The third Roger brother, Bob, was signed from New Cross, replacing Arthur Pilgrim, who planned to switch to 500cc Formula 3 car racing. The season opened with a successful National Trophy run. Plymouth were beaten in the first round, followed by Rayleigh, and then Swindon in the Division III final, but in the Second Division rounds Oxford again quickly ended the Falcons' run.

In the National League Exeter remained unbeaten at home, and would have won the championship but for injures sustained by Johnnie Sargeant, Jack Bedkober and Don Hardy. Sargeant suffered severe head injuries at Rayleigh while local youngster Maurice Barnett fractured his thigh. Despite the injuries the season finished with a flourish, the Falcons winning all but two of their last fifteen matches. Unfortunately it was not enough to overtake Poole in the championship race.

Like his brothers before him, Bob Roger was an outstanding success and along with Hardy and Gent, was called up to ride for England 'C' in the opening test match against Sweden at the County Ground on August bank holiday. A huge crowd of 11,000 turned out to watch England win 61-46. In October the highest postwar crowd of 14,000 watched a challenge match against Wembley Lions. Exeter were on course to achieve a notable victory but Goog Hoskin's engine failed in the last race, resulting in a 42-42 draw.

Bob Roger was recalled to New Cross in 1952, despite attempts by Exeter to buy him, but an influx of Australasian talent was about to arrive. Australians Jack Geran and Neil Street and New Zealander Jack Hart joined the Falcons; Hart's impact was rather brief as he broke his leg in the opening meeting. Another change saw the Third Division become the Southern League. In May Bill Dutton resigned at team manager and was replaced by Bernard 'Broncho' Slade.

The season opened with an international challenge match against a Swedish touring side, Smerderna, that resulted in a 42-42 draw. Goog Hoskin became the Falcons' top man, but the rest of the team took a little while to settle at the large County Ground track. Exeter lost the early home matches against Rayleigh and Swindon, but enjoyed enough away success to finish joint third with Plymouth and Wolves. The Falcons' run in the National Trophy was short when after beating Wolves they lost out to local rivals Plymouth.

Once again the Swedish national side rode against England 'C' at Exeter. This time the County Ground was the venue for the final test, and the Swedes arriving at the end of a hectic series were beset by mechanical problems and lost 70-38.

Kiwi Jack Hart returned in 1953 and proved to be a real thrill merchant. Ron Barrett was transferred to Birmingham and another new Australian, Bob Meyer, signed up for

The 1953 Exeter Falcons.

Exeter, along with Eric Minall from Long Eaton. Prior to the start of the season, another Australian hopeful, Roy Ether was killed in a crash during practice at the County Ground.

The Southern League championship quickly developed into a battle between the Falcons and the reigning champions, Rayleigh Rockets. Exeter pulled off a notable early away win at the Weir, but the Rockets' management protested that Jack Geran had been used illegally at reserve. Their protest was upheld and the match expunged from the records. Rayleigh made most of the running, but Exeter, with Hoskin enjoying his best-ever season ably backed by Geran and Hart, kept them in their sights. The championship race reached its climax when Rayleigh visited the County Ground in late September. The match was rained off and rescheduled for the following Monday. Meanwhile Rockets' Les McGillivray was injured and unable to ride. As he had been named in the original line-up the Rayleigh team manager wanted to switch the pairing but the ACU referee, Freddie Vigers, refused. The Rockets rode under protest and lost 60-24. The following evening a draw at Southampton gave Exeter the points to clinch the championship. Their jubilation was short-lived as three days later the Rayleigh protest was upheld and the Rockets were declared champions. Exeter, not having been invited to the hearing, appealed to the RAC, who decided that the SCB were at fault. The championship title reverted once again to Exeter, who had won where it mattered – on the track. Counterprotests followed and the matter was never officially resolved.

The Falcons also enjoyed success in the Coronation Pairs competition, which was won by Hoskin and Hardy. Exeter also reached the semi-final of the Queens Cup, but lost to Glasgow Tigers.

The increasing popularity of television brought with it a decline in support for speedway and in 1954 Exeter joined the Second Division, as a result of an amalgamation with the Southern League. This amalgamation brought with it a huge increase in travel, with matches now as far away as Motherwell and Edinburgh.

While unbeaten at home, the Exeter team failed to win at away venues. Geran toppled Hoskin from the No.1 slot, and was joined by popular Hugh Geddes. Don Hardy began slipping down the order and Vic Gent, after starting the season with the Falcons, soon moved to Plymouth and was replaced by Alf Webster.

The decline continued in 1955 when the Falcons finished bottom of the table for the first time. Although Exeter managed a surprise win at Swindon, they lost four home matches, twice to the Robins. In spite of this Neil Street and Jack Geran, who between them had scored most of the Falcons' points, had a tremendous season. Geran's lowest score in a League fixture was 11 and he achieved double-figure scores in all but one challenge match, thus beating Bert Roger's 1948 record. Johnnie Sargeant retired and was replaced by Bristol's Billy Hole.

The decline in support, which had already forced the closure of West Country rivals Plymouth among many other tracks, now hit Exeter. Bernard Slade staged various second-half attractions, including amateur racing on road machines, in an attempt to rekindle support, but it was to no avail. The Falcons' management proposed an amalgamation of First and Second Division tracks, but this was turned down and when Jack Geran decided to stay in Australia, the promoting company, Exeter Motorsports Ltd, announced that they would not be staging speedway in 1956.

No further racing took place at the County Ground until 1957 when former Falcons' favourite Cyril Roger and veteran racer Geoff Pymar launched a season of Open Licence speedway. The first meeting was held on Monday 22 July and attracted a crowd of 7,000, twice the regular attendance figure of 1955. The Falcons were represented by Jack Geran, Bob Roger, Swindon's George White, Geoff Pymar, Francis Cann and Glyn Chandler, and the opening match saw Exeter beat Norwich 58-38, despite the presence of Aub Lawson and world champion Ove Fundin in the Stars line up. Fundin returned the following week to win the

Goog Hoskin.

Jack Geran.

Western Trophy individual event with a 15 point maximum. Exeter lost 46½-48½ to Southampton in a Challenge match on August bank holiday, the dead heat was between Roger and Brian Hannan in heat 6. Riders proved very difficult to find for a Britain *v.* Overseas match a week later, and Overseas narrowly defeated the 'locals' by 50-46.

The Oxford Cheetahs won 52-44 at the County Ground on 19 August. The match was followed by midget car racing; one car crashed on the greyhound track and did so much damage that it almost bankrupted the speedway promoters. An Exeter Trophy meeting, won by Dick Bradley was held in early September, and the penultimate meeting saw Swindon gain a 52-44 victory. Rain made the track difficult and reduced the crowd to 2,500.

Another Exeter Trophy closed the season, won this time by Jack Geran, who dropped his only point to Bob Roger. Rain again made conditions difficult but the crowd numbers had doubled, allowing the promoters to at least break even.

Pymar and Roger had hoped to rejoin the National League in 1958 but their application was refused, probably due to Exeter's geographical location. When a proposed Junior League also failed to materialise, they opted to continue with open-licence racing.

The season began on Easter Monday with a challenge match again Southampton. Cyril Roger was still sidelined with a broken leg, suffered the previous season, so his brother Bob led the Falcons, who lost 53-43. Wimbledon made their County Ground debut, complete with World Champion Barry Briggs, a week later. Although Briggs equalled the track record and scored an 18-point maximum, Exeter won 51-24 with George White the top Falcons scorer on 14.

Briggs returned in May to win the Open Championship with a 15-point maximum. At this point the promotion seemed to lose its way. After a three-week break Ronnie Genz won a further Open Championship but declining crowds had apparently caused a cash-

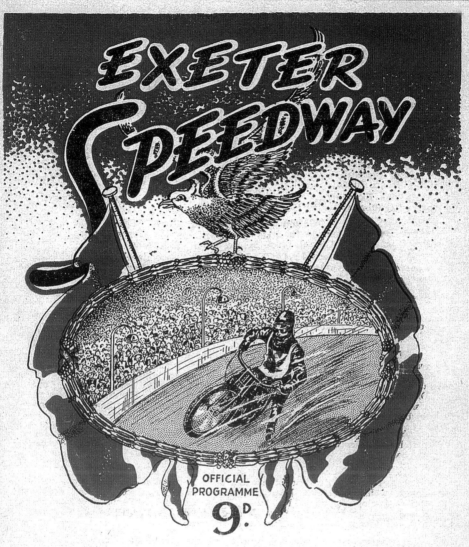

EXETER SPEEDWAY

OFFICIAL
PROGRAMME
9ᴰ·

MEETING No. 14   SEASON 1961

Provincial Riders' Championship
(SPONSORED BY REMINGTON ELECTRIC SHAVERS)

MONDAY, JULY 3rd at 7.30 p.m.

A 1961 programme cover.

flow crisis. Despite plenty of newspaper rumours, no further meetings took place until September when Pymar and Roger made one last attempt to attract the crowds.

Exeter, with former world champion Peter Craven drafted in at the last moment, beat a Midland Select 49-47 but sadly failed to attract a break-even crowd. A week later the season ended with a junior championship which, while losing money for the promoters, was won by Colin Gooddy.

No further speedway action took place in Exeter until the autumn of 1960. By then two former Plymouth riders, Wally Mawdsley and Pete Lansdale, were promoting at Rayleigh in the newly formed Provincial League and were keen to open a second track. They decided on Exeter, and using Rayleigh riders to form a Falcons team, staged three challenge matches against Bristol, Plymouth and St Austell in the autumn. Despite extremely wet weather the meetings attracted sufficient support to encourage Mawdsley and Lansdale to apply for permission to enter the Falcons in the Provincial League the following season.

Their application was accepted and the Falcons were relaunched on Easter Monday 1961. The line-up for the opening challenge against Poole Pirates consisted of Eric Hockaday, Pete Lansdale, Francis Cann, Eric Howe, Len Glover and two Australian newcomers Bob Innocent and George Summers. Exeter were beaten 41-37 by Poole Pirates so the management quickly began to make changes. The Falcons were also

Exeter riders celebrating their 1962 Knock-Out Cup victory. From left to right: Alan Cowland, Len Silver, Howdy Byford, Dennis Day, Pete Lansdale.

plagued by injuries and altogether twenty-two different riders were used. One of these was Len Silver, who signed from Ipswich in April and promptly broke his collar bone in his first match for Exeter. The turning point came when Silver returned in mid-season and suddenly hit form. He quickly became dominant around the County Ground and when veteran Howdy Byford was signed from Oxford Exeter results rapidly improved. Jack Unstead was another late-season addition and rode the last two away fixtures.

Exeter now had a formidable team and 1962 promised great things, the Falcons now tipped as possible champions. Silver and Unstead headed the team, which also included Lansdale, local favourite Francis Cann, Eric Howe, Roy Bowers, Howdy Byford and another addition from Ipswich, Dennis Day. Those hopes were short-lived, for less than three weeks into the new season, on 13 April, Unstead was killed in a track crash at Ipswich, while guest-riding for the Witches. A week later, on Good Friday, Bowers quit during a challenge match at Plymouth.

Plymouth forced a draw at the County Ground on Easter Monday but despite their growing injury problems, Exeter managed to avoid losing any further home matches. Gradually the Falcons pulled the season around with a young Londoner, Alan Cowland, coming in at reserve. By July Exeter had won away at Neath and Bradford and were clawing their way up the Provincial League table, where they eventually finished a highly creditable third behind Poole and Neath. The Falcons also enjoyed a good run in the Knockout Cup, where aided by a run of home draws they reached the final and defeated Stoke 106-86 on aggregate. To round off a memorable year, Len Silver won the Provincial League riders championship at Belle Vue.

In just two seasons, Mawdsley and Lansdale had made Exeter into one of the Provincial League's more successful and well supported teams. The riders were smartly turned out in green and white quartered shirts and white boots, and the promoters' attention to detail ensured that the track staff were equally smartly attired.

Having finished in the top three, hopes were high of doing even better in 1963 especially with Cliff Cox joining the team from defunct Plymouth. Cox, whose £130 transfer fee was paid by the supporters' club, came as replacement for Pete Lansdale, who retired from racing to become team manager. The season got underway on 1 April with a Western Cup Victory over St Austell. The second half was marred by a serious crash in which Eric Howe suffered a broken wrist and severe head injuries.

The League campaign began well with home wins over Cradley Heath and St Austell, followed by an away win at Long Eaton. The regular pattern of home wins and away defeats continued until 25 July when the Falcons drew 39-39 at Middlesbrough. A month later Exeter were further strengthened by the arrival of Jimmy Squibb from defunct New Cross. Squibb made an immediate impact with two full maximums. He scored a third on Monday 9 September but that did not prevent top of the League, Wolverhampton, from snatching a shock 40-38 victory at the County Ground. Squibb scored a fourth maximum in the Falcons' final home Provincial League match against Long Eaton, then top-scored against National League Southampton in a challenge. He dropped a rare point in a revenge victory over Wolverhampton, which, due to the non-arrival of several Wolves riders, became the Tony Sweetman Select. Squibb then teamed up with Silver to win the pairs event which ended the County Ground season.

The 1965 Exeter Falcons. From left to right: Alan Cowland, Des Lukehurst, Jimmy Squibb, Tim Bungay, Colin Gooddy, Ray Wickett, Maurie McDermott, Pete Lansdale (team manager).

Despite their strong line-up the Falcons had still not achieved the major success that they craved. In 1964 speedway was thrown into turmoil by a major split between the Provincial League and the Speedway Control Board. The SCB demanded that Provincial champions Wolverhampton should move up to boost the ailing National League. Wolves' boss, Mike Parker, the man who had launched the Provincial League in the first place, refused to comply with the Board's demand and was backed by his fellow promoters in the face of SCB threats to suspend their riders' licences.

It was in this tense atmosphere that Exeter staged the first Provincial League match of the new season, which opened on Monday 16 March with a challenge against Cradley. By defying the SCB, Exeter had staged an illegal meeting. Later in the week the Falcons went to Cradley for the return match and for the rest of the season the Provincial tracks ran outside the auspices of the Control Board.

The Falcons started the year with a strong top four – Silver, Squibb, Cox and the rapidly improving Cowland backed by Pat Flanagan, Cornishman Ray Wickett and new signing Des Lukehurst. The familiar pattern of home wins and away defeats continued until June when Wolverhampton won again at the County Ground. By then Silver had become co-promoter at Hackney Wick and left to join the Hawks, while Maurie McDermott replaced him at Exeter.

Cox broke his leg racing in a Four Team Tournament, which effectively ended his Exeter career, while Wickett missed several weeks with a wrist injury. Tim Bungay was eventually allowed to move from Poole, while the illegal use of Ronnie Genz, under the guise of 'Reg Neal', lasted just one match, but a popular signing was that of Cornish thrill maker Chris Blewett. The number of injuries and a constantly changing team left Exeter finishing in seventh place, in what was generally a disappointing year.

The winter brought a change to speedway when, as a result of the Shawcross Commission, the two Leagues amalgamated to form the British League. This new League enabled the Falcons to ride at the highest level for the first time in their history. Clearly Exeter now needed a strong side. Colin Gooddy was allocated from Oxford and proved to be a top man with a near 10-point average. He was later joined by former Falcon, Jack Geran, while Squibb took the move in his stride maintaining an 8-point average.

The Falcons finished a creditable ninth, the halfway point in the table, aided by an away win at Poole. Wolverhampton were again the only team to win at the County Ground in the League, but after another run of home wins the Falcons lost home and away to the League champions West Ham in the Knockout Cup Final.

The high spot of the season was the visit of the Russian tourists in July. A wet weekend seriously threatened the meeting and with no alternative date the test match against the West of England had to go ahead. The track was liberally covered in sawdust and a thrilling evening ensued, climaxing in Igor Plechanov breaking the 12-year-old track record in heat 13 and the West of England snatching a narrow 56-51 victory.

During the winter Tommy Sweetman, who had led Wolverhampton to victory at the County Ground on three occasions, was signed in exchange for Alan Cowland, while the former favourite Neil Street returned. 1966 saw Street and Geran riding together again for the first time since 1955, but it would be Geran's last season. Chris Blewett continued to thrill the fans, but when he was injured former Plymouth Devil Alan Smith successfully replaced him. Tim Bungay also suffered a serious leg injury in a frightening crash and Street missed the last two months with a broken ankle. These injuries allowed the Exeter management the opportunity to sign Norwegian Nils Paulson, albeit for just four matches.

Again the Falcons finished in mid-table, with both Edinburgh and Halifax winning at the County Ground in late June, at a time when the top home riders were plagued by mechanical problems. Ironically, it was between these two home defeats that Exeter scored their only away win, a 39-33 success at Cradley. West Ham again put Exeter out of the Knockout Cup, but this time it was in the first round instead of the final.

The three major individual events were all won with 15-point maximums. Coventry's Ron Mountford won the World Championship qualifying round, Norman Hunter took the Jack Unstead Memorial Trophy while Jack Geran was unbeaten in the Westward Television Trophy. The Russians made a welcome return but this time were beaten 60-48 by the full England side.

The 1967 season began with a gamble, which went wrong. Swedish star Bengt Jansson was allocated to Exeter by the BSPA on the condition that the Falcons release one of their other riders. Given the choice they preferred to rely on the older riders who had served them well the previous year. Exeter did however sign a Swede, the unknown Gunner Malmqvist, who made a promising start riding unbeaten against Poole. Unfortunately Malmqvist was recalled to Sweden almost immediately, and did not return until mid-season. His place was by another Swede, Per Ake Gerhardsson, who unfortunately was not up to British League standard.

Unable to win away from home and beaten at home by Coventry and Newport the Falcons dropped to fifteenth in the League. With the top men Squibb, Sweetman and Street unable to recapture their usual form, Geran was persuaded back but only lasted a few meetings, while Tim Bungay also made a brief return, but failed to recapture his pre-injury form. Chris Blewett had his usual run of injuries but still managed to compete in most of the matches.

After a troublesome spell trying to adapt to a Jawa machine, supplied by a sponsor, Colin Gooddy fell out with the management and quit, his place being successfully taken by Wayne Briggs. The season produced three promising juniors – Mike Cake, Phil Woodward and Laurie Etheridge. Nigel Boocock won the World Championship Qualifying Round with 15 points, while his brother Eric won the inaugural Westernapolis against a top-class field. Eric also top scored for England in their heavy 70-38 defeat by Sweden on 19 June.

Geran was again persuaded back but this time only lasted a few meetings. Tim Bungay also made a brief comeback, but failed to recapture his pre-injury form. Chris Blewett had his usual run of injuries but still managed to complete twenty-seven matches.

Malmqvist did not return in 1968 and, after prolonged negotiations, was replaced by Swindon's Martin Ashby. Overshadowed at Blunsdon by Barry Briggs and Mike Broadbank, Ashby's talent would flourish at Exeter where his arrival dramatically boosted the Falcons' fortunes and at the same time established him on the international scene. He became the first Exeter rider to appear in a World Final and was

Chris Blewett.

England's match winner in the World Team Cup. With Ashby, Briggs, Street, Sweetman and Squibb forming a solid spearhead, Exeter won all their home matches, and away wins at Glasgow and Belle Vue put them in contention for the championship. Sadly they failed to win vital matches at Newcastle and Newport and eventually finished third behind Coventry and Hackney.

Chris Blewett predictably missed much of the season through injury, but was ably replaced from Exeter's growing pool of promising young riders, in particular Mike Cake and Australian Chris Bass. They, along with Tony George and Phil Woodcock, had benefited from extra rides with Plymouth where the Falcons' promotion had launched Second Division racing.

The Russians again visited the County Ground but were convincingly beaten 51-27. Eric Boocock won the Westernapolis for the second time and John Boulger took the Westward TV Trophy, while Ashby won both the World Championship qualifying round and the Jack Unstead Trophy with 15-point maximums, and broke the track record (70.2) twice in successive weeks during August.

1969 heralded the start of a four-year period in the wilderness for the Falcons. Following his successes of the previous season, Martin Ashby would again head the line-up. He scored 366 points in thirty-three matches but surprisingly failed to reach the World Final for a second time. He was well supported by new signing Czech champion, Jan Holub, who quickly settled in at the County Ground. But although Alan Cowland and Tim Bungay returned to Exeter, replacing Street and Sweetman, the Falcons did not enjoy the same level of success. Mike Cake became a full time team member and was later joined by Phil Woodcock when Chris Blewett's 'thrill a minute career' came to a end following a crash in the World Championship round, which was won by Barry Briggs with a 15-point maximum.

The generally weaker team dropped to twelfth in the table and lost at home to champions Poole, Leicester and Swindon, but won 42-36 away at Newport. The Boocock family made it a hat-trick of Westernapolis victories, but this time it was Nigel who beat Eric for the top spot. Nigel was also successful in the Westward TV Trophy, while Ashby rounded off the year by winning the Jack Unstead memorial Trophy with a 15-point maximum.

Martin Ashby would virtually carry Exeter single-handed into the new decade. At the start of the 1970 campaign, New Zealander Bruce Cribb moved west from Poole and proved an immediate hit, but was quickly sidelined with a broken leg after a high-speed collision on the back straight with Belle Vue's Chris Pusey in the World Championship round in May. Another overseas signing was the Swede Bengt Andersson, who was injured just as he was finding his form. Andersson was later axed after missing his plane from Sweden and consequently a match against Wembley.

Ashby maintained his 10-plus average and beat World Champion Ivan Mauger for the Golden Helmet at Belle Vue. He went on to successfully defend it against Terry Betts, Olle Nygren and Mike Cake before eventually losing to Arnie Haley at Sheffield.

Although the Falcons only lost once at home they also failed to win a single away match and finished tenth. In the Knockout Cup they beat King's Lynn in the first round before going out to Belle Vue.

The 1970 Exeter Falcons. From left to right: Wally Mawdley (promoter), Wayne Briggs, Chris Julian, Bruce Cribb, Bob Kilby (on bike), Bob Coles, Phil Woodcock, Peter Ingram, John Richards (co-promoter).

Martin Ashby returned to Swindon in 1971 and in the other direction came Bob Kilby who had been allocated to Exeter by the rider control committee and was a very reluctant Falcon. Wayne Briggs was allocated back to the County Ground having left two years before. Jan Holub did not return to Britain but in his place Wally Mawdsley signed Australian newcomer Peter Ingram.

Mawdsley attempted to boost his team with other overseas signings: Tommy Bergqvist, who started well but had a drop in form and was eventually sacked after failing to return from a Swedish booking claiming that his alarm clock had not gone off, and Kjell Gimre who rode second halves but only made one team appearance. Instead Phil Woodcock was recalled full-time from Romford and his Bombers team-mate Kevin Holden was also given three outings. Bruce Cribb swept back to top the averages, while Kilby adjusted to the County Ground so well that he broke the track record. Briggs suffered a shoulder injury, which gave local junior Bob Coles an opportunity in the team before also going out with a broken leg. After a reasonable start the Falcons were among the top six but eventually finished fifteenth.

World champion Ivan Mauger became a regular and successful visitor to the County Ground winning both the Westernapolis and Westward TV Trophy.

Bob Kilby, Bruce Cribb and Peter Ingram all stayed on for the 1972 season. Wayne Briggs retired and Norwegian Edgar Stangeland was allocated in his place. Dave Hemus came from Belle Vue, with Chris Julian, Phil Woodcock and Kjell Gimre as back up. The line-up looked promising, but the first match at Belle Vue turned into a nightmare. Without former Ace Hemus, the Falcons went down 59-19. They took another hiding at Sheffield and then were beaten at home by the Tigers. Exeter gained their first British League point in a home draw against King's Lynn. While Kilby quickly regained his normal form, the rest of the team struggled; Bruce Cribb dropped from No.1 to No.6 in the ratings and Bob Coles was brought in to stem the tide, doubling up with Second Division West Ham and then Barrow. The find of the season was without doubt Kevin Holden, whose arrival from Romford marked the end of Phil Woodcock's career as a Falcon.

Exeter's final League placing of eleventh was at least an improvement on the previous season. For the second successive season Ivan Mauger won the Westward TV Trophy and the Westernapolis, while Kilby was victorious in the last staging of the Jack Unstead Memorial Trophy.

The departure of Ingram and Cribb meant that Wally Mawdsley had to make changes for 1973. New Zealander Frank Shuter was allocated to Exeter but more significant was the signing of a young American, Scott Autrey. Kilby continued as No.1 while Kevin Holden became a full-time Falcon.

The season opened with a challenge win over Poole but was followed by a run of defeats. Then to the surprise and delight of the fans Ivan Mauger was signed from Belle Vue. Needless to say the world champion did not come cheap and his contract included a clause that he would be flown to Exeter by private plane from Manchester for home matches.

Over 10,000 fans packed the County Ground for his first match on Easter Monday, which also saw the Falcons return to winning ways with a victory over Poole. Mauger's arrival did not please Kilby who was transferred to Oxford in exchange for Tony Lomas. Gradually Exeter's fortunes began to

Scott Autrey.

31

Ivan Mauger.

improve, but it was not until the end of the season that the Falcons first drew, then won away from home, ironically without Mauger. This successful late run lifted them to eighth in the League table. It was also noted that attendances had increased by over 1,000 per week.

When Ivan Mauger first joined the Falcons he predicted it would take Exeter two years to become League champions. In fact, thanks to Ivan's influence, that goal was achieved in half that time. Australian Peter Thompson was the only new addition replacing Bob Coles, who moved to Newport.

The League campaign opened with an away draw at Leicester and was followed by home and away successes against Poole, launching Exeter into an unbeaten run at the County Ground. Thompson and Shuter were both early injury victims, and in early July Australian champion Steve Reinke was flown over to replace Thompson. Reinke would provide the extra in depth strength to aid the Falcons in their championship battle with the Belle Vue Aces. Having won seven more away matches, often thanks to Mauger and Autrey achieving 5-1s in the final race, Exeter were neck and neck with the Aces. Earlier, after losing by two points at Wolverhampton, team manager Peter Oakes had protested at the Wolves' illegal use of non-contracted Ricky Day. The protest was upheld and Day's points were deducted which gave Exeter victory by 40-38 and the title.

On the individual front Kevin Holden proved a popular winner of the newly introduced *Express & Echo* Classic while Ivan Mauger won both the World Championship qualifier and the Westward TV trophy, and Phil Crump was winner of the Westernapolis.

Away from the County Ground, Mauger finished runner-up in both the World Final and the British League Riders Championship. He was also only headed at the top of British League averages by Ole Olsen.

In 1975 the Falcons found it tough to maintain their championship form. Chris Julian and Frank Shuter both retired, and Tony Lomas moved to Leicester. Veteran Geoff Mudge was transferred from Newport to strengthen the bottom end while Mawdsley signed another promising Aussie, Mike Farrell, to join Mike Sampson at reserve.

Farrell proved to be a real thrill merchant but was also accident-prone, crashing spectacularly in only his second race. Within a month Chris Julian returned to replace Sampson, who opted for a move to National League Eastbourne.

Exeter opened the defence of their title with a home win over Coventry, but soon suffered a major setback when Cradley won 48-30 at the County Ground. The management moved quickly to bring John Titman over from Australia and dropped Chris Julian to make way for him. Titman's arrival put Exeter back on course and the Falcons won all but one of their remaining home matches. Injuries also took their toll on the Falcons' progress. Holden scored his first British League maximum then broke a leg, which ended his season; Reinke was hospitalised with food poisoning and Titman cut his foot badly when he trod on broken glass in the pits. A second-half race in September brought tragedy. Halifax's Graham Plant fell and was hit by Exeter junior Bob Spelta, whose bike was launched over the fence into the crowd injuring four spectators, one seriously.

To combat the injuries, Les Rumsey was signed from Canterbury, but two vital away matches at Reading and Poole were lost. Reinke then disappeared back to Australia after a disagreement with the management concerning a missed meeting, and with him went Exeter's last chance of retaining the title. However the Falcons still played their part in deciding the final destination of the trophy, by beating Belle Vue they ensured that Ipswich won the championship. Exeter finished fourth.

Ivan Mauger finished fourth in the World Championship, after losing a run off with John Louis at Wembley. In British League racing Mauger was virtually unbeatable, going six meetings before he dropped his first point at Ipswich on 12 May and it would be August before he dropped the second. In total he scored twenty-four full maximums, and two paid, in League and cup matches. Ivan also swept the board in the individual

Scott Autrey and Poole's Christer Sjosten.

events winning the Westernapolis, *Express & Echo* Classic, Marlboro Southern Riders Championship and the World Championship round at the County Ground.

Exeter went into 1976 with a familiar-looking line-up, Mauger and Autrey again formed the spearhead, supported by Holden who had fully recovered from his fractured leg. Also back from injury was Mike Farrell, while John Titman had agreed to return for a full season, a new face, however, was that of Pietrus Johannes Prinsloo, better known as Peter. The Rhodesian, who had originally ridden for Wembley in 1971, came back to Britain as replacement for Geoff Mudge who was ruled out due in part to his high average and also a dispute with the management.

The Falcons quickly got into their stride, but two shock home defeats in the Spring Gold Cup prompted an early recall for Mudge. Farrell broke his scaphoid in the opening British League match but on his return, in June, fell in his third race and broke his wrist again, putting him out for the rest of the season. Later that evening Titman and Mudge were involved in a crash leaving Geoff with a broken arm, and Exeter minus both their reserves. To add to the Falcons' difficulties, Kevin Holden requested a transfer, having taken a dislike to the County Ground track. The Pole Kazimierz Adamczak was signed from Hull to replace Farrell but after failing to make an impression was replaced by Steve Koppe, who became a regular reserve while doubling up with National League Canterbury.

Injuries may have ruined Exeter's early promise but the Falcons still managed to finish third in the League. They were beaten by Newport in the first round of the Knockout Cup in the middle of their injury crisis, but easily defeated the Soviet Union in an international challenge. Ivan Mauger and Scott Autrey both reached the world final at Katowice in Poland. Mauger finished fourth, after a carburettor breakage while Scott was ninth in his world final debut. Ivan's consolation prize was victory in the World Long-Track final.

During the winter of 1977 Kevin Holden was granted his transfer to Poole, where tragically he was killed in a track accident shortly after the season began. Mike Farrell once again returned from injury and was joined at reserve by Peter Prinsloo who had made steady progress the previous summer. Mauger and Autrey again headed the order, with Titman in support. Two new European riders joined the Falcons: an enthusiastic Austrian, Walter Grubmüller, and the Czech international, Vaclav Verner, who missed the start of the season. Promoter Wally Mawdsley also made a considerable effort to sign American Bruce Penhall, but he opted for Cradley instead, thus depriving Exeter of a future World Champion.

The Falcons opened the campaign with a challenge against Polish touring side Stal Gorzow. Verner proved an immediate hit and went on to score seven maximums but Grubmüller was not so lucky; a broken arm, a damaged shoulder and finally a fractured thigh meant that he missed much of the season.

It was another tremendous year for the Falcons, but their title challenge made a slow start. Their first away win came at Birmingham on Silver Jubilee Day in June, and Coventry and Belle Vue both won at the County Ground before the tide began to turn. Twenty-four hours after the second defeat Exeter won 45-33 at Leicester. Six further away wins and three draws followed, by which time the Falcons were battling with the

White City Rebels for the championship. Exeter went to Hackney needing to win their penultimate away match to stay in the hunt. Victory was within their grasp as Mauger and Autrey led the final race for what promised to be a match winning 5-1, but the Hawks' Barry Thomas swooped around the Exeter duo to win both the race and the match for Hackney. Had Exeter won, they would have been champions, but despite a 53-25 victory at Belle Vue the title went to White City. Ivan Mauger won his fifth world individual title in rain-soaked Gothenburg, but at a price to Exeter. Mauger insisted on taking a two-week break to prepare for the championship, and missed a home meeting against Leicester. At the start of the New Year Exeter transferred him to Hull for £12,000.

This obviously was a blow to the Falcons' hopes for 1978 as Titman had also left to join Leicester. However these moves made it possible for Autrey to stay at the County Ground along with Verner, who was joined by his brother Jan. Farrell, Koppe and Rumsey, back again in Exeter colours, filled the lower orders with Norwegian Reidar Eide coming in part exchange for Titman. Eide, despite a fiery relationship with the Exeter management, had a sensational season which included sharing the track record with Autrey. Unfortunately Koppe frequently had to miss matches as his commitments with Canterbury took priority, and without a consistent reserve Exeter dropped to seventh in the League table.

Coventry were the only side to take points from the County Ground and the Bees also gave Exeter a tough time in the first round of the Speedway Star Knockout Cup. The two sides drew on aggregate, but Exeter won the replay, eventually losing to Belle Vue in the semi-final. The Falcons won their group in the early season Gauntlet Spring Gold Cup and went on to beat King's Lynn in the final. The Stars took revenge by defeating the Falcons in the final of the Inter-Divisional Cup. Even without Mauger the Exeter fans had plenty to cheer about in the Golden Jubilee World Final at Wembley where Scott Autrey finished third with Jan Verner also reaching the final, scoring 5 points.

The end of the season saw the departure of the popular Mike Farrell, Eide and Rumsey. Farrell's replacement Czech Ales Dryml made an instant impression. Dryml appeared in Exeter's last two British League matches and won the *Express & Echo* Trophy in his only appearance at the County Ground in October.

The Verner brothers and Dryml were joined by fellow-countryman Zdenek Kudrna for 1979 so it was little wonder that the Falcons became known as 'Czechxeter'. Autrey remained the unchallenged No.1, Prinsloo returned for his fourth season while veteran Nigel Boocock, who doubled up with Canterbury, became Exeter's sole Englishman.

The season began with home and away wins over Poole in the Spring Gold Cup. Several away wins were recorded in the British League but with so many foreign riders in the side Exeter all too often found themselves short-handed due to continental commitments. King's Lynn was the only team to win at the County Ground and the Falcons managed to finish fifth overall, two slots better than 1978.

Autrey was ruled out of the World Championship as the result of a dispute with the American authorities, but went on to top the British League averages and set a new County Ground track record of 66.2 seconds, which would stand until 1992. Zdenek Kudrna qualified for the World Final in Poland and finished a creditable fourth.

Exeter enjoyed another good Knockout Cup run defeating Belle Vue and Swindon before losing to Hull in the semi-final. The Falcons also missed out to the Vikings in the final of the Inter-League Four-Team Championship at Sheffield.

As the seventies came to a close so too did Exeter's fifteen seasons as a first-division team. Shortly before Christmas it was announced that the Falcons had been withdrawn from the British League because of declining attendances and the cost of maintaining a top-class team. The promotion's accountants reported a £50,000 loss on the season, before the sale of riders was taken into account. The news came as a total shock to the supporters but Exeter's future was not in doubt for long as team manager Peter Oakes agreed to take over as promoter and promptly relaunched the Falcons as a National League team.

The switch of Leagues meant that Oakes had to build a completely new team. The only Exeter rider to move between Leagues and decades in 1980 was Nigel Boocock who became No.1 and captain for what was to be his last season in British speedway. Australian Robert Maxfield was signed on loan from Belle Vue while John Barker was purchased from Eastbourne. The task of assembling suitable second strings would keep Oakes busy for the rest of the season. Only 18-year-old Martin Hewlett of the original contenders would see the season out. Neil Farnish, Bob Watts, Mike Sanderson, Phil Vance, Gary Flood, Tony Garrard and locally based Tony Sanford were all given opportunities along with Former England International Arnie Haley who was later sacked after failing to appear for a home meeting. In August Ellesmere Port's John Williams became available and Oakes quickly snapped him up. Another latecomer was Dave Brewer who was signed from Wimbledon and retained his team place for the rest of the season.

The 'fledgling' Falcons were seriously tested when powerful Newcastle won the opening National League fixture at the County Ground, but Exeter won all but three of their remaining matches. Away from home the Falcons achieved victories at Canterbury and Workington, and a draw at Milton Keynes. Probably Exeter's greatest achievement in that first season of National League was simply surviving!

Many fans resented the loss of British League racing and stayed away despite Oakes' wholehearted efforts to promote the Falcons. Not surprisingly the venture lost money, but Oakes' determination did not waiver.

That winter, Wally Mawdsley, who had remained as co-promoter, sold out to Reg Fearman of Poole Stadium Ltd, who formed a new partnership with Oakes and his wife Pam. 1981 saw another team reshuffle. Boocock retired to Australia, leaving Maxfield, Barker, Hewlett and Williams as the basis of the team. Australian Les Sawyer was signed from Halifax while Oakes purchased Andy Campbell from Reading for a bargain £500. At a junior free-for-all practice session, Oakes spotted two youngsters, Keith Millard and Kevin Price, who would eventually join an increasing array of new talent with included Brewer, Sanford and Williams's cousin, 15-year-old Simon Cross. Campbell had to wait until Barker injured his knee before getting a chance in the team at Glasgow where he scored ten paid 11.

The Falcons improved five places from their previous season's twelfth and remained unbeaten at the County Ground. On their travels Exeter won at Workington, Rye

House, Milton Keynes and Scunthorpe. John Barker was dropped when he asked for a transfer after being pulled out of a ride in Mildenhall, and was replaced by former Falcon Bob Coles, who signed on loan from Weymouth.

The season was marred by the tragic death of Tony Sanford following a second-half crash at the County Ground on Monday 7 September. Tony, a popular local rider, is to date the only rider to lose his life while racing at Exeter. A benefit match was staged in which Exeter Past and Present was beaten 46-38 by Bruce Penhall's Select.

The following winter Robert Maxfield left for Ellesmere Port, John Williams retired to concentrate on his motorcycle business and Martin Hewlett returned to Swindon. John Barker settled his differences with Oakes and returned to the line-up forming the spearhead with new skipper, Les Sawyer and Bob Coles, backed up by Keith Millard, Andy Campbell and Dave Brewer.

Injuries would play a major role in the Falcons' 1982 fortunes as both Sawyer and Barker were hurt at Glasgow in May. Barker returned quickly but then fractured his scaphoid at Canterbury, which finished both his season and his Exeter career. Sawyer's dislocated shoulder also limited his appearances and it was left to Coles, Campbell and Millard to carry the team for the rest of the year. Brewer soon called it a day and was replaced by Swindon junior Steve Bishop. Mark Reeve made a brief appearance before being forced out with fractured ribs in his second outing. Second halfers, Mike Semmonds, Michael Coles and Tim Fey were given team opportunities as the injury list grew and in the final match at Crayford, Alun Rossiter made his first appearance as No.8.

Despite the injury crisis the Falcons lost only to Mildenhall and Newcastle at home and even won away victory at Oxford. Andy Campbell represented Exeter in the National League Riders' Championship, where he finished eighth and also set a new scoring record with 439 points.

Peter Oakes' efforts to develop a successful youth policy paid dividends in 1983. Robert Maxfield returned to the County Ground and along with veteran Bob Coles provided the expe-

Tony Sanford.

The 1983 Exeter Falcons. From left to right, back row: Verner (coach), Bob Coles, Rob Ashton, Alun Rossiter, Kevin Price, Pete Thesiger (team manager). Front row: Steve Bishop, Rob Maxfield, Keith Millard.

rience which allowed Oakes to fill the side with exciting young talent. Alun Rossiter now joined Steve Bishop as a full-time Falcon while Keith Millard was given the No.1 race jacket. Campbell left to try his luck with British League Poole. Kevin Price, who had signed as a 16-year-old two years earlier, also returned but new signing Marcus Williams crashed in his first race at Newcastle and was subsequently paralysed. Another new face, Australian Rob Ashton, arrived in time for the Falcons' home Knockout Cup win over Canterbury and from then the team was virtually settled. It proved to be 'a middle of the road' side, losing home matches to Middlesbrough and Berwick, but only once won away, at Canterbury. The Falcons again finished tenth in the League, but the season was best remembered for their Knockout Cup victory. Having disposed of Canterbury Crusaders home and away in the first round, the Falcons next beat Rye House. In the semi-finals they met powerful Mildenhall and amazingly defeated the Fen Tigers 74-21 at the County Ground and successfully held on to their advantage in the away leg to earn a place in the final against local rivals Weymouth. In the home leg the Wildcats held Exeter to a meagre 9-point lead, but a brave performance at Radipole Lane 24 hours later saw the Falcons win the Cup on aggregate by a single point.

Keith Millard won the British Junior Championship at Canterbury and Bob Coles celebrated a well deserved testimonial. The year ended with an appearance by Ivan Mauger and new German World champion Egon Müller.

Earlier in the season Oakes had announced his intention to take the Falcons back into the British League in 1984. This would require around £20,000 and by the autumn the fundraising was going so slowly that the future of Exeter speedway was yet again plunged into doubt. At the eleventh hour the Falcons managed to purchase Leicester's British League licence when their Blackbird Road stadium was suddenly sold for redevelopment. A winter of frantic activity followed as stadium improvements were carried out and Oakes battled to assemble a team. Les and Neil Collins were included in the Leicester deal but both refused to join Exeter. Talks to secure the services of Andy Graham, Bobby Schwarz and Larry Ross also failed, so Oakes was eventually given special permission to track Ivan Mauger for home matches only. The basis of the team would be Andy Campbell, Sean Willmott, Robert Maxfield and a newcomer from Denmark, Frank Andersen. A string of riders including Keith Millard, Leif Wahlman (tragically killed in the Under-21 final at King's Lynn), Stefan Deser, Frenchman Patrice Blondy and Kent Noer were given opportunities and altogether twenty different riders appeared in the Devon Air Falcons race jacket. Two of the most popular were American Bobby Robinson and Louis Carr, whose stay was cut short by a broken ankle. Sadly nothing worked and Exeter eventually finished second from bottom in the table having won just eight and drawn two out of their thirty matches. The British League revival was a financial catastrophe for promoter Peter Oakes and his family, and he quit after five years of hard work and commitment.

During his spell as promoter Peter Oakes had launched the Interline Imps junior team to give his up-and-coming riders opportunities to race occasional challenge matches. In 1984 the Imps contested the British Junior Knockout Cup. Having battled through to the semi-final where they achieved a surprise away win at Ipswich, the Exeter juniors then comfortably beat Milton Keynes home and away to take the title. Sadly the Imps' victory was overshadowed by Oakes announcement that he would not be continuing.

Again the future looked bleak but once more salvation was at hand. Colin Hill, one of Oakes' local shareholders, believed that the Falcons could still be financially viable if they returned to National League racing, and bought Oakes out. Few believed that the inexperienced Hill would find success in 1985 where the ultra-professional Oakes had failed. Hill, a supporter of 25 years, had no knowledge of speedway management other than one season as a shareholder. He quickly assembled an experienced management team, which included Ron Byford as team manager, announcer Bob Radford and track manager Ted Lethbridge. The purchase price included the contracts of Robert Maxfield, Steve Bishop, Kevin Price, Michael Coles, and Mike Semmonds. Nigel Sparshott was quickly snapped up from Oxford as a potential No.1, and when Boston folded preseason, Hill signed Colin Cook. The big surprise of the season proved to be Kevin Price, a last-minute addition to the side, who went on to become Rider of the Year.

The new-look Falcons, sponsored by a local motorcycle firm, Bridge Garage, soon got into the groove with a run of home wins, including a first defeat of eventual

New promoter Colin Hill meets Colin Cook (left) and Nigel Sparshott (right).

champions Ellesmere Port. Exeter were also leading at Barrow in the Knockout Cup when the floodlights failed, the match was abandoned and the Cumbrian track closed.

The 1985 season was generally considered a success despite a total lack of away wins but it proved a costly year for Colin Hill. He admitted losses in excess of £9,000, so economies would be made for 1986 especially as Bridge was not continuing its sponsorship. Robert Maxfield had retired, and although Sparshott looked set to continue, he suddenly changed his mind and quit, while in a cost-cutting exercise Cook was loaned to Boston.

Rain forced the cancellation of several early matches but it quickly became apparent that the team was extremely weak and when new signing Bruce Cribb was injured, Hill was forced to recall Colin Cook and away success was finally achieved at Canterbury. Alan Rivett and Alan Mason joined the Falcons mid season and results began to improve. The August bank holiday meeting was rained off, bringing Hill's financial problems to a head, but help arrived in the form of sponsorship from ex-Oxford team manager, Roger Jones. At the end of the season Ron Byford left to become full time speedway manager at Swindon and was replaced Exeter's clerk of the course, John Brooks. Colin Hill introduced the *Express & Echo* Rangers in 1986 to give experience to his juniors.

The 1987 team showed little change from its predecessor. Steve Bishop moved to Arena Essex while Kevin Price joined Long Eaton. Into their places came David Smart from Swindon and Honiton-based David Gibbs on loan from Poole. Gibbs initially rode at reserve, in preference to Tony Mattingly and Andy Sell, and made a big impression when he scored paid 15 against Swedish tourists Smerderna, as replacement for Alan Rivett who was late returning from Australia.

Disaster hit in an early Grand Slam qualifying round when Bruce Cribb and Poole's Steve Schofield crashed heavily with one of their bikes bouncing over the safety fence into the crowd, leaving Cribb with head, neck and knee injuries. The Falcons' away fixtures started well with a victory over Glasgow at Workington but sadly this result was wiped out when the Tigers withdrew from the National League. It would be Exeter's only away success.

Even without the injured Cribb, who after a brief comeback missed the rest of the season, the Falcons consistently won at home, until Cook crashed and was also injured in a match against Arena Essex, which the Hammers won 44-34. To add to Exeter's difficulties David Smart broke his ankle at Rye House and was out until August. Rivett damaged shoulder tendons in that match but continued to ride. Gibbs lost his place to Alan Mason who returned in June, but a month later was axed when he refused to go north with the team.

Without Cribb, Kevin Price was recalled, but he too failed to recapture his old form and Exeter eventually finished third from bottom, their worst ever National League placing. The one bright spot for the Falcons was the arrival on the scene of North Devon grass-tracker Peter Jeffery who won the inaugural South West Junior Championship.

Clearly the Falcons needed strengthening but efforts for 1988 proved disappointing. Bruce Cribb returned while the crowd's favourite, Dave Trownson, signed from

Edinburgh, came south along with Brummie Paul Evitts. Colin Cook was appointed captain, backed by Rivett, Andy Sell and Tony Mattingley, while Jeffery waited in the wings.

Cook started well before breaking his ankle, Cribb never got going and eventually retired while Evitts failed to live up to expectation and was sacked, which resulted in him taking legal action. The Falcons continued to struggle, and Richard Green was signed from Mildenhall as a second string. Green proved to be a real racer and won the hearts of the fans with a spectacular drive around Gordon Kennett in his first meeting. Trownson finally recaptured his form against Milton Keynes but then broke his thigh in a crash which ended his racing career.

Team manager John Brooks pulled off a master stroke in July by persuading Steve Regeling to the join the Falcons, giving Exeter the No.1 rider they had needed so badly for so long.

The winter brought behind-he-scenes problems. Prolonged wranglings over riders deals saw Hill take control of the negotiations himself, and bring back Dave Trownson this time to replace Brooks as team manager. With Regeling and Green confirmed as starters for 1989, Hill then sprang a major surprise by also bringing back Frank Andersen, who had dropped out of speedway after riding for Coventry in 1985. With Cook, Jeffery and Sell confirmed, Hill had a team that promised much for Exeter's forthcoming Diamond Jubilee season.

After a shaky start the Falcons got into their stride and in the second home League match thrashed Middlesbrough 76-20. A month later Exeter suffered a record 78-18 drubbing at Berwick. The big home wins continued but it was not until mid-September that the Falcons finally won away at Long Eaton. Victory over the invaders was followed by a last heat win at Mildenhall and a draw at Milton Keynes. This memorable finish lifted Exeter into fifth place, their highest ever National League placing. Earlier the Falcons had enjoyed a thrilling Knockout Cup run. Having beaten Rye House and Stoke they drew on aggregate with Berwick but lost out to the Bandits in a tense replay. Exeter also reached the finals of the Fours where they finished third overall behind Peterborough and Stoke.

Frank Andersen's second spell as a Falcon lasted just one season, and in 1990 he was transferred to Peterborough. After a winter in Australia, Peter Jeffery moved up to join Steve Regeling and Richard Green as third heat leader. Colin Cook and Steve Bishop were the second strings with Mark Simmonds joining Andy Sell as reserve.

The traditionally wet press day saw Cook fall and fracture a collar bone, but amazingly the popular racer from Felixstowe bounced back to score 11 in the opening challenge match against Long Eaton. The National League campaign began badly with a run of defeats. Hill was openly criticised for releasing Andersen, and things got worse when Exeter were edged out of the Knockout Cup quarter-final by Wimbledon. Exeter also lost out to the Dons in the Fours qualifying rounds when Wimbledon pipped them for a Finals place in the last round at Poole. Regeling and Peter Jeffery provided the Exeter fans with some compensation by taking the runners-up spot in the Speedway Star Pairs Championship at Glasgow.

The most talked-about matches of the season were two bruising encounters with Ipswich. At the County Ground Regeling tangled with Dean Standing in an incident

Steve 'Frog' Regeling (right) with fellow Aussie Craig Boyce.

Steve 'Frog' Regeling (right) with fellow Aussie Craig Boyce.

which also brought Andy Sell's Exeter career to an end. Later Green was involved in an on track altercation with Chris Louis. The Falcons won but the Witches' venom was directed at Green. In the return at Foxhall it was soon apparent that the Ipswich riders were targeting him and sure enough Shane Parker was excluded for sending the Exeter favourite hurtling through the back straight fence, fortunately without serious injury.

Hill and Trownson attempted to boost the Falcons' fortunes by replacing Colin Cook with the former National League Riders Champion, Ian Barney, but Barney failed to adapt and Cook soon returned. Peter Jeffery's season ended abruptly on August bank holiday, when he suffered a fractured thigh. This not only ended his season also ruled him out of the Falcons late tour to Poland where they raced a team match at Lezno and took part in an individual meeting at Bydgoszcz where Green and Regeling finished second and third behind a young Tomasz Gollob.

The 1991 season was one of confrontation for the Falcons. The winter had seen a reconciliation between the top level British League and the stronger and more successful National League. The agreement saw four National League sides given the chance to move up to First Division level. Poole, Wimbledon, Ipswich and more surprisingly Berwick all made the switch.

Colin Hill, disillusioned by the winter developments which drastically reduced the strength of the National League, decided to quit and put the Falcons up for sale. Three buyers showed interest but none matched Hill's valuation. He eventually appointed former Milton Keynes and Long Eaton promoter, Roger Jones, as manager and left him to get on with building the side while he, Hill, concentrated on his property business.

Jones swiftly reached agreement to keep skipper Steve Regeling at the County Ground. Several leading National League riders had moved up with their teams and Regeling found himself the National League's No.1 rider. Equally quickly it became clear that Jones did not want Richard Green, which upset his many fans. After a traumatic few weeks Green eventually signed while David Smart arrived on loan from Swindon for a second spell at the County Ground. Colin Cook, Peter Jeffery and Mark Simmonds all

The 1989 Exeter Falcons. From left to right: Peter Jeffery, Colin Cook, Richard Green, Steve Regeling, Andy Sell, Alan Rivett, Frank Andersen.

returned but unfortunately Frank Smart could not be fitted in as reserve due to a new assessed 6-point average so was replaced by grass tracker Richard R. Knight.

The Falcons lost their first Gold Cup match at Hackney on Good Friday. But Jones shrewdly noticed that the Hawks were tracking Aussie Dave Hamnett who did not have a work permit. The Exeter manager slapped in a protest, which was upheld, and the result amended in Exeter's favour. It proved to be the Falcons' only away win of the year. The Falcons finished third in the Division Two Gold Cup but the Fours was an abysmal failure for Exeter and it was during this competition that the first signs appeared of a squabble that would develop into open conflict between the Falcons riders.

With League and cup results not going Exeter's way, Jones announced that he would quit following terrace criticism. The fans' main cause for complaint surrounded his controversial pairing of Regeling and Green at 1 and 2. Jones claimed that this gave Exeter a potent opening partnership, but the supporters did not agree. The next falling-out occurred when David Smart, after an impressive start to the season, suffered a spate of mechanical problems, which drew criticism from Jones. The manager, meanwhile, had sorted out similar problems for Colin Cook, and persuaded him to continue at the County Ground.

Big home wins over Middlesbrough, Edinburgh and title-chasing Glasgow, were achieved in July and hopes were high that the Falcons would continue their winning ways against Newcastle. Unfortunately a bad crash saw Richard R. Knight tangled up with three bikes and seriously injured. The evening ended with further disappointment as the Diamonds sneaked a last-heat maximum to win 45-44.

Still unable to use Frank Smart, Jones signed Justin Elkins on loan from Poole. League leaders Arena Essex overcame a seriously overwatered track to snatch a 46-44 victory at the County Ground. The controversial manager, who had personally prepared the track, then saved the Falcons from a wasted trip to Peterborough where the cash-strapped Panthers were refusing to ride until they were paid. Jones collected the turnstile money and duly if unconventionally sorted the situation out.

The summer of discontent ended with several junior meetings which drew criticism from the senior riders.

Colin Hill took charge of the Falcons himself in 1992 and Roger Jones returned to Milton Keynes after the BSPA persuaded Hill to take over the ailing Knights. Steve Regeling was transfered to Middlesbrough and into his place came 1989 world finalist Tony Olsson from Reading. Paul Fry was signed from Long Eaton. Peter Jeffery took over as captain, and Green, Cook, and Simmonds were all retained. Sadly Frank Smart's average once again ruled him out and he moved to Milton Keynes. The line-up was completed by the arrival Ian Humphreys from Arena Essex.

County Ground action: Colin Cook, Steve Regeling and Poole's Craig Boyce.

Richard Green.

The Exeter season opened with an international against Rospiggana, Olsson blew his engine to smithereens and the visitors won. The Gold Cup started with encouraging performances at Stoke and Rye House, although the latter was marred by several crashes which left Fry and Jeffery injured. Jeffery was lucky to escape serious damage when he fell and an opponent rode over his head! Exeter won at Long Eaton with Green scoring a 18-point maximum.

The new-look Falcons were giving cause for cautious optimism, and the League campaign began in tremendous fashion on the May bank holiday with the Falcons sweeping Middlesbrough aside 54-36 and Olsson breaking Scott Autrey's 13-year-old track record with a time of 66.1 seconds. Sadly it would be Olsson's sole League appearance for Exeter as Hill's other track, Milton Keynes, had run into serious financial difficulties and had been closed down. One of the repercussions was that Reading demanded early payment of statutory loan fees for Olsson and Hill had no option but to release the hugely popular Swede. Without him Exeter achieved a second win at Long Eaton which would prove to be the Falcons' last away victory for four years. Frank Smart took Olsson's place in the team but the hope was gone. Exeter went out of the Knockout Cup after failing to hold on to a 26-point first-leg lead at Stoke and also lost at home in the League to Glasgow and Peterborough. The Peterborough match saw teenage Jason Crump, rejected by Hill at the start of the season, score paid 16, to rub further salt into the wound.

Richard Green managed to give the fans something to cheer about when he finished third in the League Riders Championship at Coventry.

The season ended with Colin Cook staging a well deserved benefit meeting at the County Ground in which newly crowned world champion Gary Havelock took part, while the supporters expressed their disappointment by voting Tony Olsson Exeter's Rider of the Year.

The Rangers won the 1992 reserve League thanks in the main to Scott Pegler and Tony Palmer. Graeme Gordon managed an illegal debut with them, when he was still only 15 years old.

If 1992 had ended in disappointment then 1993 promised to be even more depressing. During the winter the BSPA announced a new pay scale, which failed to meet with the approval of the riders. It was rejected by Colin Cook, Peter Jeffery and Richard Green so with the BSPA deadline looming, Hill assembled his team earlier than ever before. Heading the line-up would be former World No.2, Gordon Kennett who remained on Hill's books following the collapse of Milton Keynes. Kennett led a side made up of Paul Fry, Mark Simmonds, Ian Humphreys and Frank Smart with the addition of Reading's David Steen. Scott Pegler and Tommy Palmer filled the reserve berths, but many supporters considered the team too weak. Practice day was a disaster: Fry walked out, Kennett never appeared, and Palmer and Steen were delayed by traffic.

Swindon won an opening night challenge, with Peter Jeffery in their line-up. Fry and Green returned in time for the first home League match against Rye House, but by then Steen was already out having partially severed his thumb in his chain.

Glasgow and Peterborough both won at the County Ground and a long term back injury forced Humphreys to retire from racing. Smart broke his wrist at Swindon and then, shortly after making his international debut for England against Sweden at the County Ground, Green broke his neck in a simple fall. Although the extent of his injury was not realised at the time, his career was effectively over. Fry broke his ankle long-tracking and Green's replacement, Rob Woffinden lasted just two matches before he too was injured. Fry came back from injury but fell out with Hill over missing a match at Sheffield to allow him to compete in the world long-track final in Germany. Meanwhile Kennett left under a cloud when Hill signed Vaclav Verner. The Czech favourite returned for just eight matches before he too was injured.

This was Exeter's worst season under Hill, as the Falcons finished tenth out of eleven. The team may not have shone but there were still moments of glory. The test match in which Sweden narrowly beat England and Joe Screen broke the track record was a tremendous success and attracted a huge crowd while West Country Television not only sponsored the Westernapolis, won by Glasgow's Robert Nagy, but also televised it as an hour-long programme.

Sadly life became even tougher for the Falcons in 1994, with Hill remaining determined to stick to his budget, he started the season without an established No.1 rider. With Kennett gone, Green still injured, and Simmonds seemingly retired, Exeter once again took on a cosmopolitan appearance. Verner returned, bringing with him a promising young Czech, Antonin Svab junior, and Dutch grass tracker Henk Bangma who were joined by Austrian champion Andy Bossner. Paul Fry patched up his differences with Hill, and Tommy Palmer and Scott Pegler continued as reserves.

Once again the team was extremely weak, and Nigel Leaver was quickly signed, sadly with little effect. Exeter lost six straight League matches before recording their first victory of the year over Oxford on May bank holiday. Bangma was axed shortly afterwards, much to Hill's regret as he believed the Dutchman could make it given time, and Leaver also departed having failed to make an impression. As a replacement Hill signed exciting Finnish prospect, Mike Pellinen but he only lasted six matches before a serious crash with fellow countryman Vesa Ylinen in Exeter's home win over Edinburgh ended his career. That match saw Mark Simmonds return to the side, but Fry injured his wrist and he was subsequently sidelined for two months.

More defeats followed, although a victory over Newcastle gained the Falcons their only bonus point of the season. The mercurial Bossner quit and returned to Austria then Svab was injured whilst racing in Germany and missed the rest of the season. Four weeks later on August bank holiday Verner was injured and the same day David Smart, Bossner's replacement also crashed out.

Guest riders helped Exeter beat Newcastle, Oxford and Edinburgh, and Peter Jeffery also made a brief comeback but it would be to no avail. The Falcons needed a result against fellow strugglers Sheffield but only managed to draw and as a result finished bottom of the table for the first time since 1955.

The two divisions amalgamated in 1995. In theory the idea might have worked, had a small group of first-division promoters not moved the goalposts by insisting on keeping all their top riders instead of allocating them to second-division tracks. Colin Hill, faced with some serious team building, surprised his critics by signing the top Brit Mark Loram on loan from King's Lynn. On Verner's recommendation he also signed two more Czechs, Bo Hadek and Pieter Vandirek. For the rest of the team Hill depended heavily on his Second Division survivors, Verner, Svab, and Mark Simmonds while Fry again signed at the last minute. With Pegler ruled out by the averages, Graeme Gordon was named as reserve.

Despite the presence of Loram, Exeter struggled, going six matches before they achieved their first win. Loram broke the track record at Edinburgh and scored an 18-point maximum at Sheffield. Their first win came against Middlesbrough and then more importantly Wolverhampton were defeated in a last heat decider thanks to a superb ride by Paul Fry who beat world champion Sam Ermolenko. Reading drew at the County Ground when Loram missed a flight from Poland. Vandirek missed most of the season due to two broken wrists and having lost the last six matches the Falcons were again condemned to finish bottom of the table.

During 1995 Hill agreed to run a team in the fledgling Conference League. The team would be known as the Devon Demons, and their race jacket would carry the emblem of the old Plymouth Devils. To begin with, Hill staged The Demons' matches on Thursday evenings, but two meetings a week not only upset the neighbours and but also failed to attract viable support. When the Falcons went out of the Knockout Cup in the early stages, Hill was able to ulitilise Mondays for conference League fixtures and attendances quickly exceeded the break-even point. Although the Demons did not win many matches the team gradually began to unearth talent. Scott Pegler and Graeme Gordon proved the main stays, while Roger Lobb, Paul Fudge and Paul Oughton came through and eventually earned themselves regular spots with the Falcons. Others like Kevin Phillips and Richard Ford provided reliable back up.

To prevent a third wooden spoon and expulsion from the Premier League Exeter clearly needed support for Mark Loram. Hill unsuccessfully attempted to sign Tomasz Gollob before five times world long-track champion Simon Wigg offered to join the Falcons. Vandirek finally returned from injury while Svab moved to Middlesbrough allowing former Falcon Michael Coles to be signed from Oxford.

Loram missed the start of the season due to a suspension for missing a test series at the end of the previous season but the Falcons began with a shock win away at Poole in the Easter Trophy. Simmonds was injured in a World Championship round and Vandirek was forced out by recurring problems with his wrists. Both riders had started the season well. German Jörg Pingel was signed on Wigg's recommendation but soon dropped in favour of Alun Rossiter. Rossiter was injured at the County ground, prompting a return for Peter Jeffery. Exeter achieved their first away League victory since 1992 when they won at Middlesbrough and also gained a second success at Poole, this time in the Knockout Cup in which they reached the semi-final following a draw at Swindon. The Falcons climbed four places off the bottom to finish fifteenth, and Wigg ended the season on a high by winning the Grand Prix Challenge in Prague.

By the end of 1996 it was obvious that the Premier League was still split between the old first and second-division teams. When the split finally took place, Colin Hill opted for the financially viable Premier League rather than the more expensive Elite League. Hill's decision was considerably influenced by a £39,000 loss on the '96 season, despite very good crowds.

Mark Loram.

The return to the lower level for 1997 meant the departure of Mark Loram and Simon Wigg which upset the fans who had enjoyed seeing the world's top riders in action every week. Loram was prepared to stay at the County Ground and race in the Premier League but this was vetoed by the BSPA.

Another departure was that of skipper Paul Fry. The usual winter indecision ended abruptly when Hill signed Leigh Lanham on loan from Ipswich, and Fry was sold to newcomers Newport. Paul was joined at Queensway Meadows by Roger Lobb, who joined the Wasps on loan. Michael Coles was appointed captain, and the heat-leader trio was completed by a surprise return of Frank Smart. Peter Jeffery, Graeme Gordon and Paul Fudge completed the six man line-up. Mark Simmonds was left out of the team at this stage as doubts remained as to his fitness.

The season opened with the Richard Green Benefit Meeting, a hugely successful event won by Joe Screen. The Falcons had a early wake up call when Long Eaton won the opening Knockout Cup match at the County Ground launching what would be a season long debate regarding the legality of softening the regulation hard compound tyres. While the Falcons soon got back into the winning groove, away wins still eluded them.

In the Premier League success was easier to come by, and wins were recorded at Stoke and Berwick. Eighth place in the final table was good enough for the Falcons to qualify for the newly constituted Young Shield competition. In the opening round

Exeter overcame Reading and met Newcastle in the semi-final. Although the first visit of the Diamonds was rained off, Exeter were again successful even though Coles and Gary Lobb, who had replaced Fudge, missed the first half of the match at Brough Park. Bad weather delayed the home leg until the last week of October, so having overcome the Diamonds the Falcons faced Long Eaton in the final two days later. Having held the Invaders to a 10-point lead the Falcons staged the home leg on Thursday 30 October. The Falcons wasted little time in wiping out the Invaders advantage and Gary Lobb became the hero of the hour sweeping around the opposition as the Falcons went on to win Hill his first major trophy. Earlier, Coles and Lanham had finished third in the Premier Pairs Championship.

For 1997 the Conference League rules demanded that competing teams staged twelve home matches. This was far too many than could be fitted comfortably into the Exeter fixture list so Hill joined forces with Tim Stone, at newly opened Newport to form the Western Warriors. The Warriors successfully raced their first six home matches at the County Ground before the team switched to the Welsh track to compete the season. This would be Hill's last foray into Conference League racing as declining relations with his County Ground landlords made it impossible to stage extra fixtures.

For 1998, Exeter were forced to release Leigh Lanham to comply with the points limit, which enabled Mark Simmonds to return. Paul Oughton replaced Gary Lobb as reserve while Roger Lobb was recalled from Newport. The Falcons began the League campaign with a draw at Newport before eventually recording away wins at Berwick and Stoke. Despite an early home draw with the Isle of Wight, the Falcons went on to finish third, their highest ever placing under Colin Hill. Coles and Smart went one better by finishing second in the Pairs Championship at Newport. Exeter also qualified for the Fours at Peterborough, but did not progress beyond the semi-final. The future was threatened in May, when Hill was robbed of the night's takings after a home match in May. Already shocked by a drug-related attack away from speedway Hill handed over the team manager's duties to Tony Lethbridge, and concentrated on the administrative side of the business.

Peter Jeffery ended the season with a successful testimonial but Frank Smart shocked Hill by asking for a transfer.

Hill resumed as manager in 1999, having decided against taking over St Austell during the winter. Unfortunately the points limit ruled out Roger Lobb, who went on loan to Arena Essex. Cornish youngster Chris Harris signed for Exeter on his 16th birthday after a successful first season with the Gulls in the Conference League. Joining him at reserve would be one of the Falcons own discoveries, Chris Courage. Courage sadly did not make the grade and by mid-season was losing interest. Hill moved quickly and replaced him with Wayne Barrett, who had dropped out of speedway in the eighties after riding for Poole. An early casualty was Peter Jeffery who sustained several back injuries in a crash at Reading in April and did not race competitively again. Harris meanwhile made a successful debut for Young England against Sweden at the County Ground.

The first away Premier League win came at Berwick and a month later the Falcons won on the Isle of Wight, but hopes of a third victory at Glasgow were dashed by a 2-

point defeat. Roger Lobb returned to haunt his old team when the Arena Essex Hammers ended their long unbeaten home run in July. A month later the Hammers were back and won again, this time ending the Falcons' Knockout Cup hopes in the semi-final.

Further disappointment followed in October when Newport forced a draw at the County Ground, ending Exeter's hopes of reaching the Young Shield final for the second time in three years. But it was clear that Hill was already planning his 2000 team when Seemond Stephens, another St Austell discovery, announced that he had signed

Mike Coles.

for Exeter. He would join Michael Coles, by now the Falcons' all time top-scorer, Mark Simmonds and Graeme Gordon. Roger Lobb made yet another return, and Bobby Eldridge completed the line-up on loan from Eastbourne, to join Harris as reserve in a line-up not universally rated by the pundits or fans.

But the team clearly showed that they were supremely strong at home. While the Falcons failed to win away from home, a run of big home wins ensured them of all the bonus points before rounding off the qualifiers with a historic 75-15 whitewash of Arena Essex. The Premier League began in similar vein with another fourteen 5-1s against Glasgow before Tiger's guest Scott Swain managed to edge Harris out of second place in the final heat.

In no time the Falcons were sitting at the top of the League table for the first time since anyone could remember. The big scores and the bonus points continued but despite several close calls the first away win was not achieved until Stoke in August. A second win at Berwick was followed 24 hours later by a draw at Glasgow. The last week of the season saw several teams still in with a chance of winning the title but Exeter held on and completed a clean sweep of bonus points in a narrow defeat at Workington to clinch the championship. The Falcons went on to reach the finals of the Premier Trophy and the Young Shield but lost to Hull and Swindon respectively. The Robins also beat the Falcons in the semi-final of the Knockout Cup. The season ended with a victory parade through the streets of Exeter and a civic reception at the Guildhall.

For 2001 Colin Hill retained the basis of his championship side. Chris Harris moved back to Cornwall where St Austell had become Trelawny and Lawrence Hare joined the

Falcons from Oxford. Another former Gull Jason Prynne came in at reserve along with an untried Ipswich junior, David Osborne. Osborne was soon replaced by Matt Cambridge, who after only a handful of matches fractured his thigh at Hull. Eldridge also missed much of the season through injury and Hill used no fewer than eleven different riders at reserve before the arrival in mid season of Krister Marsh. Marsh quickly settled in and played an important role in Exeter's two away wins at Trelawny and Reading. These successes lifted the Falcons right back into contention for a place in the Young Shield where they were eventually lost to the Isle of Wight in the first round. Nail-biting matches against Swindon and Reading earned the Falcons a place in the Knock-

Mark Simmonds.

out Cup final against Hull. The hero of these matches was Lawrence Hare who twice overtook opponents on the last lap of his final race to put Exeter through.

A month later, at the end of November, Hill was shocked to be called in by his County Ground landlords and told that due to a major redevelopment of the stadium by the rugby club speedway would not be able to continue in 2002. This unexpected eviction came just a few days before Hill was due to attend the BSPA conference at which he must declare Exeter's intention to run the following season. Undeterred by the situation he consulted his lawyers and as a resulted confidently announced that he intended to stay on at the County Ground until his lease expired at the end of the 2004 season. His stance was backed to the hilt by the supporters who launched a 'Keep the Falcons Flying' campaign. This attracted overwhelming support from speedway fans throughout the country as a result of which a 5,700-signature petition was handed in to Exeter City Council calling for speedway to be allowed to continue. Faced with such dignified and well-organised opposition the rugby club's plans crumbled, and agreement was eventually reached whereby the Falcons would continue to race at the County Ground until the end of 2002 and Hill would accept compensation for the remaining two years of his lease.

The uncertainty meant a late start to Hill's team building. Skipper Mark Simmonds, Bobby Eldridge and Matt Cambridge all re-signed, Roger Lobb agreed to return after completing his period of suspension and Krister Marsh was happy to continue on loan. During the period of uncertainly Seemond Stephens had signed for Trelawny, and for a time it looked as though Lawrence Hare too would be lured to Cornwall until Hill persuaded him to stay with the Falcons. That left one place to fill and after the usual winter stand-off Hill and Michael Coles finally agreed a new deal during Lew Coffin's 80th birthday party at Yeovil.

The new season opened with West Country rivals Trelawny inflicting a shock home Premier Trophy defeat on the Falcons. Although Lobb and Marsh rode well the three Exeter heat leaders lacked the speed and sharpness of Seemond Stephens and Richard Wolff who notched 24 points between them. Further home defeats followed as Swindon and Newport won at the County Ground.

On Sunday 14 April the Falcons travelled to Newport where they suffered a tragic blow when Lawrence Hare clipped an opponent's back wheel and was paralysed in the resulting fall. The shell-shocked Exeter team bravely returned to action the following evening and achieve their first win by defeating League newcomers Somerset Rebels.

The Premier League began with another home defeat, as Stoke won 47-43, but gradually the Falcons returned to winning ways. Their efforts were not helped by an increasing number of injuries. Michael Coles, Mark Simmonds, Matt Cambridge and Bobby Eldridge all had spells on the sidelines but nevertheless Hull Vikings were the only other team to win at the County Ground. For the first time since 1995 the Falcons failed to win away from home and this eventually cost them the chance of a place in the Young Shield.

Throughout the summer enormous efforts were made to raise funds for Lawrence Hare and the season culminated with the all-star Hare Raiser Classic. This proved to be a glorious success and was won by Scott Nicholls. Lol himself made an emotional return to the County Ground and the meeting raised almost £25,000. By the end of the year the Lawrence Hare Support Fund stood at a magnificent £145,000.

Colin Hill had spent much of the year locating a new base for Exeter Speedway. When the rugby club failed to fulfil their compensation agreement Hill announced that he intended to stay on at the County Ground until his lease expired in October 2004.

ALPHINGTON

When the Second World War ended in Europe in May 1945 a small group of local enthusiasts led by Frank Buckland, Bernard Slade, and business man Bill Eastmond, decided to celebrate by staging a speedway meeting. With no stadium available due to the County Ground still being in military hands after serving as an army camp for both British and American troops during the conflict, permission was given to hold the event at Exwick playing fields. Thus the European Victory Meeting, which took place on Whit Monday, was in effect a grass track event albeit the 360-yard circuit was liberally coated in sawdust due to heavy rain the previous night.

The main event was won by Fred Tuck while a local rider, Clifford Plain, was victorious in the junior class. The meeting attracted 8,000 spectators and raised £200 for the St John Ambulance. Encouraged by their success the promoters decided to build their own temporary track on land off Alphin Brook Lane at Alphington where they could stage regular racing until the County Ground became available again.

The 250-yard track was constructed in just a fortnight and the first meeting took place on Thursday 5 July. It still officially being wartime, the promoting company, Exeter Speedway Motor Club, was threatened with a 'ploughing up' order by the War Agricultural Committee but the first meeting still managed to go ahead with an all star line-up which included Ron Johnson, Fred Tuck, Mike Erskine, Roy Clarke and Vic Warlock plus locals Bernard 'Broncho' Slade and Reg Robins. On a dry cinder track the racing produced clouds of dust but that did not deter Johnson from winning all but one of his heats and the final. He also established the track record at 63.2 seconds.

A week later that record was smashed no fewer than five times before it was finally credited to Oliver Hart at 61 seconds. The event was a Pairs Championship but the sparse records of the time did not record the winners. The same applies to the England v. Dominions match which took place the following week, other than that Hart again broke the track record; his time was 58.2 seconds.

Heavy rain caused a match between Devon v. the Rest to be called off at tea time on 26 July, but a second England v. Dominions match on 2 August resulted in a 39-32 home win. Former Wembley star Colin Watson was persuaded out of retirement for this meeting by Frank Buckland and promptly top scored for England with 12 points.

The penultimate match of the short summer series saw the North and South draw 39-39. Finally the season ended on 16 August with the official ACU Southern Championship. A crowd of 7,000 or 8,000 people watched Bill Kitchen win an all action final from Eric Chitty who overslid and took Ron Johnson into the fence, which due to wartime shortages was constructed from turf and top soil taken from the track.

This would be the last public match at the hastily built Alphington track but it would continue to host the Exeter Falcons' Tuesday morning practice sessions until the early 1950s.

Vaclav Verner.

In 1951 it was replaced by another purpose-built training track constructed behind the Peamore Garage on the main A38 Plymouth road. This proved a popular venue for junior racing on Sunday afternoons. Although no official meetings were staged the racing still attracted plenty of spectators. Exeter's Don Hardy also held regular training schools at the track. Sadly the venue was short-lived due to complaints about noise from local residents.

Practice also took place at Dulditch on Woodbury Common. The site had been a temporary wartime Royal Marine camp and the track was a rough oval cut out of the gorse and bracken. Another popular venue with Falcons' riders for winter practice sessions in the early '50s was the beach at Dawlish Warren, where more than one machine was badly damaged by an unscheduled excursion into the sea.

HALDON

Britain's first permanent long-track circuit opened at Haldon racecourse overlooking the Exe estuary on Sunday 8 October 1978. The project was the brainchild of Exeter promoters Wally Mawdsley and John Richards along with team manager Peter Oakes. The 800m track had been laid out on the infield of the Devon and Exeter steeplechase course and the opening meeting attracted an enormous crowd, officially numbered at 15,000. In fact so many people turned up that cars overheated while queuing on the notoriously steep Haldon Hill and the organisers had to send extra gatekeepers to various parts of the perimeter to catch punters coming over the hedge.

The Falcons' Norwegian star Reidar Eide won the opening meeting from Phil Crump and Peter Collins. Crump would dominate racing at Haldon and the following year won both the international events staged there. On Sunday 13 May 1979 he finished ahead of Ole Olsen and Bruce Penhall and then returned on 30 September to take his second gold medal ahead of Bruce Cribb and Vaclav Verner. The programme for that meeting also included the Anglo-American dirt bike challenge in which the world road-racing champion Kenny Roberts competed against speedway champion Peter Collins on Yamaha 750cc dirt bikes. To complete a full day's racing Bernie Leigh won the national class from Steve Ryding and Martin Goodwin. But despite the big crowds the project began to run into financial difficulties and the situation was not helped by seemingly endless disputes with the ACU who claimed responsibility for long-track racing in Britain. Hopes of staging World Championship events were dashed when following an inspection by Charles Ringblom on behalf of the FIM the promoters were told that the track must be increased to 1000m before an international licence would be issued. Sadly this was not possible due to the close proximity of the horse-racing track.

Nevertheless a full programme of events was planned for 1980 culminating in a big international meeting on August bank holiday. The Haldon season was scheduled to start with a national event on Sunday 29 June. It was a poor choice of date as not only were all the top riders competing in the Commonwealth Final of the World Championship at Wimbledon that evening but the Falcons were also racing away at Stoke. Only around 1,100 fans turned up and the meeting was a financial disaster. Both events, the international and national, were won by Andy Grahame. In the former he finished ahead of Steve Bastable and Kenny Carter, and in the twenty-rider national event Grahame won in front of Mike Garrad, with Carter again third.

Sadly it was the end of the line for long track in Devon and for Long-Track Racing Associates, as the directors took legal action against each other to recover outstanding debts. A year later it was announced that the directors would not be renewing their lease and the track was demolished. Not only was the long track itself lost but also the frequently used 300m speedway training track. The site had also included a utilised part of the long-track pits bend. Well-attended training and practice sessions were held during the two winters often under the guidance of Jack Geran.

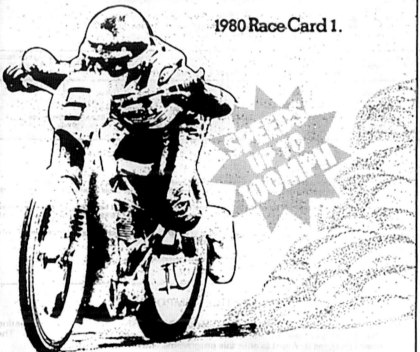

A 1980 programme cover.

PART II

PLYMOUTH

PLYMOUTH

Speedway racing reached Plymouth on Saturday 13 June 1931 at the Pennycross Stadium at a time when Exeter was just about to close down. Pennycross had first been used for greyhound racing in May 1928 and the following year it was rumoured that a speedway track would also be constructed. Those rumours did not become reality until Western Speedway Limited, fronted by former rider Freddie Hore, showed interest in 1931 when the 413-yard circuit was finally built.

Plymouth's riders in the first challenge match against Exeter were Bert Spencer, Bert Jones, Maurie Bradshaw, Noel Johnson, Peter Slade, Spencer Stratton and George Preston. Disappointingly only 6,000 spectators saw Mrs P. Fletcher, the wife of one of the directors, cut the tape to open the track. The new promoters had anticipated a larger attendance but early rain may have put off many prospective supporters; nevertheless it was considered it a satisfactory start. The *Western Morning News* commented: 'Those who had not previously witnessed dirt track racing were thrilled and bewildered as the grotesquely attired riders dashed by, "broadsiding" around the corners with handlebars almost at right angles to their machines and blinding one another with flying sand.'

Plymouth won the opening match 32-21, but Exeter had the more spectacular riders, particularly Buster Buckland. However, Plymouth's Spencer Stratton proved equally spectacular in the semi-final of the Handicap event, when he took a tumble and was stretchered off with concussion. Reg Robins, from Honiton, won the final, ahead of Will Coleman and George Preston.

Tuesday was designated as Plymouth's pre-war race night, and although mention was made in the *Western Morning News* that Bristol would be the visitors on 16 June, the meeting did not take place. Instead Plymouth rode away at Exeter, where they were beaten 33-20 with Noel Johnson top-scoring at his former track with 7 points. The next meeting at Pennycross saw Plymouth narrowly beat Lea Bridge 26½-25½, with Maurie Bradshaw and Jimmy Stevens finishing in a dead heat for first place in their second race. Bradshaw also won the handicap final from team-mate George Preston.

Plymouth enjoyed a more comfortable victory over Southampton whom they beat 30-24 in a match which produced plenty of good racing and several crashes. Bert Spencer won his first two races before missing out to Saints' Norman Parker, who scored a 9-point maximum. Spencer also set what would be fastest time of the season, 81.4 seconds in the opening heat. An unofficial Exeter team returned to Plymouth on 4 August as racing at the County Ground had by now ceased, thus only locally based riders took part. Johnson scored a maximum against his old team, and Spencer too rode unbeaten as Plymouth won 40-13 on a poorly prepared track. Exeter's Buster Buckland won his first race and then suffered two engine failures. It was suggested that he would be joining the Plymouth team, but the move never materialised.

West Ham were the next visitors. The Hammers were defeated 27-24 on 18 August. A rain-soaked track made for slow times, falls and plenty of machine trouble. In the final of the Golden Helmet, Spencer's tyre came off on the third lap, but he still managed to finish second behind Noel Johnson, who completed a hat-trick of wins. It proved to be the little Australian's last victory as a week later he suffered fatal head injuries during the seventh heat of Plymouth's match against Coventry. He fell while lying third and was hit by one of the visiting riders who was unable to avoid him. The 24-year-old Johnson was taken to the South Devon and East Cornwall Hospital where he later died from his injuries.

A second match against Southampton was rained off on 1 September and the wet weather was still prevalent a week later when, in difficult conditions, Wimbledon beat Plymouth 38-16. Bill Clibbett and Stan Lemon were unbeaten for the Dons, who totally outclassed Plymouth, but the visitors' rough tactics drew complaints from the crowd and the riders were accordingly warned by the ACU steward. A novelty eight-heat match between the married and single riders was staged in the second half which the Bachelors won 26-20!

A 10,000-strong crowd saw Plymouth suffer a second heavy defeat the following week. This time the visitors were Stamford Bridge who won 35-18. This match was run in fine weather and the Pensioners riding was described as 'supreme'. Plymouth returned to winning ways before an equally large crowd on 29 September when they beat Lea Bridge 29-24. Bert Spencer topped the Plymouth scorers with 8.

The beginning of October saw High Beech win 29-25. The crowd for this meeting dropped to 6,000, but this was probably due to a power cut which blacked out much of Plymouth prior to the meeting. The power returned just before start time, but more rain made for very poor conditions. West Ham made their second appearance at Pennycross on 13 October. Once again the track was very wet but still produced good racing. This time the Hammers won 33-21. During the evening a collection raised £15 12s towards a memorial trophy for Noel Johnson.

The inaugural season ended with a match again the star-studded Crystal Palace team who stormed to victory 36-17. Without doubt this was the best line-up seen at Plymouth as the Palace team included Joe Francis, Harry Shepherd, Nobby Keynes, Triss Sharp and Tom Farndon, who broke the track record with a time of 79.2 seconds. He later won the Golden Helmet final. Cyclone Billy Lamont rode in the second half but was hindered by engine troubles and was subsequently beaten by both Bert Spencer and Farndon in match races. Local man 'Francis Drake' won the junior race.

Plymouth's successful first season encouraged Western Speedway Ltd to apply for membership of the newly formed National League in 1932. Art Warren, Bert Jones, Bill Clibbett, Bill Ellmore, Frank Pearce, Jack Barber, Jimmy Ewing, and Stan Upton formed the basis of the Plymouth Tigers team but altogether twenty-two riders would be utilised including Bert Spencer, Ted Bravery, Phil Hart and Peter Slade.

The *Speedway News* clearly did not rate the Tigers among the contenders for honours: 'Latest newcomers, Plymouth, have got together a band of riders who are frankly well known, but who would scarcely obtain a place in a strong team. Coventry did well last year, Plymouth may do the same but frankly I think not.'

The season opened with a challenge match again Southampton on 31 March. It was immediately apparent that Plymouth were in for a tough time. The Saints won 36-17 in a long drawn-out meeting which did not finish until 10.15 p.m. The delays were invariably caused by machine problems for the home team. In heat 2 every rider suffered an engine failure causing the race to be restaged later in the programme, while heat 7 was rerun five times due to falls or engine problems. A week later Wimbledon won 31-21 at Pennycross in a match which attracted 10,000 fans. Again Plymouth suffered numerous engine failures.

The National League had been formed to encompass the various regional Leagues which dated back to 1929. The new League would be run as two separate contests, the National Speedway Association Trophy and the National Speedway League Championship. Crystal Palace were the first visitors to Pennycross in the former competition on 12 April and won 37-16. That defeat was followed by a 36-15 drubbing by the Wembley Lions and, more encouragingly, a single-point loss to Stamford Bridge, 27-26.

A new local development was a signal system whereby a rocket would be fired into the sky 30 minutes before the start time at Pennycross and three rockets in the event of a postponement.

On Tuesday 3 May yet another London team was victorious at Plymouth. This time the victors were the West Ham Hammers, who won 33-20. Cecil Smith, the secretary of the Speedway Promoters' Association, was present to offer assistance and advice to the Plymouth management, while Wembley's manager, Johnnie S. Hoskins, offered to send down one of his top mechanics to oversee the newly hired Pennycross workshop staff. During the interval Hoskins' 6-year-old son Ian gave a demonstration on his miniature bike.

Despite these offers of help, the defeats continued. Belle Vue won 28-25 on 31 May and a week later a crowd of 10,000 saw the Tigers lose to Stamford Bridge. A further defeat came at the hands of the Kangaroos in a challenge match on 14 June, but victory was finally achieved the following week when Coventry were beaten 34-20. Success, however, came at a price, as skipper Frank Pearce fractured his arm when hit by another bike. A second victory was achieved on 28 June when Sheffield were convincingly defeated 39-14.

Two weeks later Plymouth raced Clapton in the first round of the National Trophy knockout competition. The 11,000 spectators were unhappy with some of the steward's decisions as the visitors won 50-44 over sixteen heats. The Tigers' Eric Collard was flagged off after two false starts due to the visiting riders lagging behind in the rolling starts, and Lupton declined to ride in the rerun as a protest, leaving Norman Parker and Alf Foulds to ride around alone accompanied by the jeers of the crowd. In another heat Plymouth's Jack Jackson mistook a signal to slow down to avoid a fallen rider and in so doing let Parker pass him. The highlight, for Plymouth fans, was the race in which Bert Spencer finally managed to beat Parker. Clapton went on to win the second leg 63-29.

Plymouth finished bottom in both tables, winning just two Association Trophy matches, but doing slightly better in the National League where the Tigers achieved home victories over Coventry, West Ham, Stamford Bridge and Clapton.

The season ended on 11 October with a sixteen-heat match between England and the Rest. The Rest, which included Vic Huxley, Ron Johnson and Bluey Wilkinson, won 58-36. Their reserve was future world champion Lionel Van Praag who failed to score.

The Plymouth Tigers found life just as tough in 1933. The length of the track was reduced to 388 yards, and Mr P. Fletcher replaced Freddie Hore as team manager. Plymouth would again track twenty different riders among them Frank Goulden, Ted Bravery and Jack Jackson who had all been retained from the previous season, plus Bill Clibbett, Frank Gould, Jack Sharp, Austrian Leopold Kilmeyer, Sebastian Roth from Germany, Mick Murphy, Reg Stanley, John Glass, Harry Bray and Bill Stanley. League matches were now run over nine heats and the scoring system changed back to the 4-2-1 system used in 1929.

Despite a heavy 42-20 home defeat at the hands of Clapton in the opening League match Plymouth fared a little better than the previous summer recording victories at Pennycross over Belle Vue, Coventry, Wembley, Crystal Palace, Sheffield, Nottingham and West Ham. The Tigers also achieved their first away success when they won 45-18 at Coventry, and came close at Sheffield before losing 32-31. Despite their successes – one match attracted a record 20,000 attendance – the Pennycross outfit still finished a lowly ninth, one place above bottom team Nottingham. Plymouth also went out of the National Trophy in the preliminary round to Coventry who beat the Tigers 119-106 over two legs.

The Tigers' struggle continued in 1934. The new electric starting gate now replaced the early hand-operated device which had appeared the previous year. The Plymouth team once again consisted mainly of Australians, Jack Sharp, Bert Spencer, Frank Pierce and Mick Murphy along with Bill Clibbett, Ted Bravery, Bill Stanley, Ben Living and Phil Hart. The Tigers made an encouraging start, drawing 26-26 with Harringay, and then beating Wimbledon 27-22 before newcomers New Cross Rangers won 31-23 at Pennycross. Once again the Tigers finished one from bottom having come very near to closure at one point during the season. However the management succeeded in keeping the track in operation even though Plymouth pulled out of the National Trophy after beating Lea Bridge 29-22 in the first leg of the preliminary round. Clearly the track was in trouble and the following year it would be taken over by Jack W. Colebach.

In a bid to put the speedway back on a viable financial footing Colebach opted for a season of open-licence racing in 1935. He also changed Plymouth's nickname to the 'Panthers' but retained their orange and white colours. The gates reopened on 17 July with an evening of individual racing watched by a crowd of 3,500. Tiger Lewis won the main Raven Trophy event while Harvey was the winner of the Plymouth Distance Handicap.

An unofficial England *v.* Australia fixture was the next event and at the beginning of August the Hackney Wick reserve team were beaten in a challenge match with local rider Francis Drake replacing Hackney's Reg Stanley who failed to appear. Cornish grass trackers Ivan and Tommy Kessell were billed to race in the junior event against Exeter's Bernard Slade.

The Panthers recorded further challenge successes over Southampton, Cardiff and Eastbourne before losing to a London select. That match was ridden under a cloud and the flag flew at half-mast as a mark of respect for British champion and Plymouth track record-holder Tom Farndon who had died following a crash at New Cross. The season ended on 10 September when Bert Jones won the ten-heat Plymouth Trophy in front of a mere 2,500 crowd.

Attendances may not have been high but were clearly sufficient to encourage Colebach to relaunch League racing at Plymouth. For 1936 a genuine Second Division, known as the Provincial League, was formed to replace the Reserve League which had earlier been attempted. Plymouth joined Bristol, Southampton, Nottingham, Liverpool and Cardiff (who made an early withdrawal) in the new division. 'Cyclone' Billy Lamont returned to Pennycross where he joined Dicky Case, Les Bowden, Jack Hobson, Les Gregory, Les Bowden, Jack Bibby, Fred Tuck, Don Hemingway, Sammy Marsland and local favourite Francis Drake in a familiar looking line-up.

The new season got underway at Pennycross on Tuesday 5 May and once again the Panthers failed to achieve success. In the Provincial League they managed to win just two of their sixteen matches, which included a 47-25 victory over the eventual champions, Southampton. The Saints later took revenge by winning 43-29 on their second visit in September. In the Provincial Trophy the Panthers drew 34-34 against the West Ham Hawks at the Custom House. This was the Eastenders' second team and Plymouth were forced to use two Southampton riders, Cliff Anderson and Jimmy Riddle, when Lamont and Wise failed to arrive in time.

The season ended at Pennycross with Plymouth's Australian riders beating a USA team 56-52. Jack Bibby top scored for the Aussies with 11 points while America's Cordy Milne rattled off five wins before falling last time out. Manuel Trujillo scored 11 points and Pee Wee Cullum 10. The USA team also included stunt rider Putt Mossman.

After another season of disappointment and poor results Plymouth's future was again uncertain. That uncertainty continued until May 1937 when it was reported that a 'London company' was preparing to relaunch speedway racing at Pennycross and the opening meeting would take place on the eve of the Coronation of King George VI. The meeting actually took place slightly earlier on Tuesday 12 May and featured a representative England *v.* Australia test match as the main attraction. Between 4,000 and 5,000 people turned up to watch this encounter which resulted in a 27-27 draw. Former Plymouth riders Bill Clibbett, Ted Bravery and Stan Dell rode for England while the strong Australian side included Billy Lamont, Dick Case and Vic Duggan. England's George Dykes, then skipper of Nottingham, collided with Jack Sharp, their machines tangled and both riders somersaulted down the track. After receiving attention from the St John Ambulance Brigade the riders were able to continue, but the rerun was put back and became the final race at which stage England led by 2 points.

The second-half individual event for the Coronation Cup was won by Billy Lamont. Although it was reported that an unnamed London company intended to run further events, none seem to have taken place, and no further track action took place in Plymouth until after the Second World War.

Plymouth was still recovering from the devastation of enemy bombing when Southern Speedways Ltd, a company formed by Peter Bantock, Jack Austin, team manager Gordon Parkins and promoter Jimmy Baxter, decided to re-introduce the cinder sport to the naval city. Fortunately Pennycross Stadium had avoided serious damage and speedway quickly became a major attraction for the war-weary Plymouthians. Like Exeter, Plymouth was seen as an ideal venue for Third Division racing and the first meeting took place on 24 April 1947. The post-war era opened with an individual event, the Lord Mayor's Trophy, which was won by Southampton's George Bason with a five-ride maximum. The first meeting was marred by first-night gremlins and a host of engine problems. New promoter Jimmy Baxter described some of the difficulties as 'a combination of over-anxiety on the part of the riders and a lack of energy on the part of our gallant "pushers-off" '.

The new team was to be known as the Devils and the line-up consisted of Billy Newell, nicknamed the Iron Man, Cornwall's Ivan Kessell, Stan Lanfear, Alex Gray, Vic Gent, Charlie Challis, Harold Sharpe, Doug Bell, Bill Deegan, Jimmy Cashmore, Ralph Westwood, Bill Sale, Des Tamblyn, Len Covell and Ken Slee. Their new race jacket would be yellow with a red devil emblem. The Devils' nickname did not please Ivan Kessell who was a committed Christian and lay preacher. He hated the Plymouth race jacket and took it off whenever he could.

Devon rivals Exeter and Southampton rode challenge matches at Pennycross at the start of May with the Falcons winning 48-33 but the Devils claimed their first team victory when they beat the Saints 47-37. On Thursday 15 May Plymouth rode their opening National League Division 3 match against the Tamworth Hounds at Pennycross. Sadly, despite 11 points from Devils' Stan Lanfear, it was the Hounds who narrowly took the League points 43-41. This set the pattern as the Devils lost six more home matches and failed to register a single win on their travels. Plymouth's first home League success did not come until 5 June when Wombwell were defeated 43-40. The fans then had to wait until 7 August for their team's second success. Once again it was the unfortunate Wombwell Colliers who went down 54-29 in the 'B' match. By that time diminutive Len Read had joined the Devils from Norwich. Len only stood 5ft high and claimed that when he first walked out the supporters thought he was the mascot. The remainder of the season brought further victories over Hanley, Tamworth, Cradley Heath, Exeter, champions Eastbourne and a 42-42 draw with Southampton.

Altogether the Devils used twenty-four riders as the season was spoilt by a string of injuries. Consequently Plymouth finished bottom of the eight-strong League but that did not stop a crowd of 15,636 turning out to see the Devils beat their arch-rivals Exeter 47-36 in the Devon Derby on 23 October. Although Plymouth won on the night Exeter still took the silver trophy, donated by the supporters' club, on aggregate.

The Devils enjoyed better results in 1948. Pete Lansdale, Peter Robinson and Bonnie Waddell joined the team which still included Billy Newell, Ivan Kessell, Alex Gray, Vic Gent, Charlie Challis, Len Read, Ken Slee, Ted Gibson, Wally Matthews and Bill Sobey. Lansdale and Robinson made an immediate impact while Newell resigned the captaincy after a poor run of form and Challis disappeared from the scene altogether.

Plymouth Speedway

Souvenir Programme

of the

FINAL SPEEDWAY MEETING

Season 1947

October 23rd

Proceeds of this Meeting will be donated as follows :—
50 per cent to local Hospitals
50 per cent to Printers' Pension Fund

OFFICIAL
PROGRAMME

PRICE
ONE SHILLING

A 1948 programme cover.

Action at Pennycross.

The all-time record crowd of 20,000 filled Pennycross for the season's opener, the John A. Chapman Trophy meeting on Good Friday, won by the Devils' skipper Billy Newell.

Plymouth started well with a challenge match victory over Southampton but then lost heavily at home and away to Exeter in the Devon Derby. The Devils also made a quick exit from the National Trophy, beaten 106-98 on aggregate by Cradley Heath. The National League campaign began with a home draw against Tamworth and a week later Plymouth achieved their first post-war away win when they beat Coventry 45-37. The Bees, Stoke, Wombwell and Hull were all comfortably beaten at Pennycross, but on 1 July the old enemy, Exeter, arrived in Plymouth and ended the Devils' unbeaten run. Rivalry between the two clubs was intense especially after two of the Plymouth bikes were discovered to have sugar in the fuel tanks at an earlier meeting at the County Ground.

A second home defeat was sustained in mid-August when Southampton, at the time locked in a desperate battle with Exeter for the League championship, won 45-38. Plymouth did their best to influence the outcome of the title race a fortnight later when they became the only team to win at the County Ground that season. Both sides were hit by injuries while the Devils took full advantage of the Falcons' mechanical problems to snatch a 43-41 victory. Plymouth almost made it two away wins on the trot the following evening at Hastings before eventually going down 44-40. Exeter however gained full revenge when they returned to Pennycross later in the season and won again, 46-38, before going on to win the championship. The Devils nevertheless had climbed out of the League cellar and ended the season seventh out of twelve.

Plymouth were to have a sucessful year in 1949. The Devils' top three, Robinson, Lansdale and Read, were joined by two important new signings, George Wall, a bulldozer driver, and Alan Smith. Both made a big impact but in the final analysis in it would be Plymouth's lack of reliable reserves which would cost them the chance of overcoming Hanley and Yarmouth and taking the championship.

Once again the Devils made an early exit from the National Trophy, this time at the hands of Devon rivals Exeter. In the League Plymouth suffered an early home defeat by Poole and later were beaten at Pennycross by Halifax Dukes while eventual champions Hanley forced a draw. On their travels Plymouth won twice at both Rayleigh and Oxford, gained revenge by winning at Poole and were also victorious at Swindon and Liverpool.

Lansdale enjoyed a superb season and ended the year as the Third Division joint top scorer with Yarmouth's Billy Bales. Bales made a huge impression at Pennycross in June when he knocked two full seconds off the track record. The Plymouth officials demanded that his engine should be checked. This was done and the motor declared perfectly legal.

The Devils eventually finished third in the League table and were rewarded with promotion to the Second Division. Despite the success of the team the management were concerned by the declining level of support.

In 1950 Plymouth quickly settled into the Second Division without any serious strengthening. While Edinburgh and Ashfield tracked world-class stars like Jack Young and Ken Le Breton, the Devils merely brought in Bill Thatcher from their sister club Southampton and still managed to win their first eight home matches. It was not until Glasgow arrived, with Ashfield and the White Ghost himself, Ken Le Breton, and won 47-37 that the Devils suffered a home defeat. Plymouth were beaten twice more at Pennycross but by much closer scores, Edinburgh 43-40 and Cradley Heath 44-40.

On their travels it was a different story but Plymouth still scored two remarkable victories. The first came at Walthamstow on 3 July when the Devils won 43-40 and then even more remarkably at Cradley on 14 July where the high flying Heathens were trounced 56-28.

Pete Lansdale.

The win at Dudley Wood was the high spot of the season and also the watershed as from then on the Devils struggled to track a full side. Cecil Bayley who had ridden eleven matches for the Devils returned to Southampton, and Bob Wigg was loaned to Exeter where he was almost immediately injured. Denis Hayles, who came in from Banister Court, was plunged straight into the Devils' line-up at reserve and, although not afraid to give it a go, found life extremely tough. Another youngster, Wally Mawdsley, was signed from Norwich at the end of August but failed to make an impression.

Worse was come in September when Johnny Bradford fractured his skull and Bill Thatcher suffered back injuries, a broken nose and facial cuts just two days before his wedding. Veteran Bronco Slade was signed from Exeter but was not allowed to ride as the move was made after the 31 August transfer deadline.

At the end of the season the Devils were unfairly demoted following pressure from other mainly northern promoters who did not like Plymouth's 'geographical location'. This in reality was the beginning of the end for the Devils, as crowd dissatisfaction followed the consequent loss of their top riders: Pete Lansdale was transferred to Walthamstow, while Peter Robinson and Len Read moved to Liverpool.

A further consequence of Plymouth's relegation was the departure of Jimmy Baxter who quit as promoter. He was replaced in 1951 by Freddie Parr, while former Exeter and Poole rider Sid Hazzard became team manager but Freddie Frappe continued as track manager. George Wall, Alan Smith and Bill Thatcher, all of whom had come up through the Devils' ranks, now became heat leaders. Johnnie Bradford was signed from St Austell and George Craig was later brought in from Swindon. Support came from Dennis Hayles, Frank Wheeler, Tom Turnham and promising local youngster Brian Hitchcock.

Plymouth again lost to Exeter in the opening round of the National Trophy, and the Devils also failed to progress in the one off Festival of Britain trophy competition. It was a slow start in the League as well. Having beaten Cardiff, Plymouth lost at home to Exeter by a single point, 42-41, and were also beaten at Pennycross by Poole, Swindon, and Rayleigh while Aldershot drew 42-42. To add to their difficulties Thatcher suffered a fractured thigh in July but a very useful replacement was found when Ron Barrett joined on loan from Birmingham, and the Devils produced a surprise result by beating the champions-elect, Poole Pirates. Plymouth also managed to record four away wins, twice at both Wolverhampton and St Austell. The Devils also lost to Exeter in the Devon Derby but won international challenge matches against Norway and the USA.

The Devils demotion had a seriously detrimental effect on attendances. In a bid to restore interest Sid Hazzard attempted to bring more variety to meetings. He attempted to introduce sidecar racing and with help from Plymouth-based junior Brian Hitchcock, a fitter in the naval dockyard, he built several midget racing cars for which he staged special meetings, one of which took place on Boxing Day that year. St Austell's Norman Street proved to be one of the top drivers.

By comparison the 1952 season would be far more successful for the Devils. Thatcher recovered from injury and Lansdale made a welcome return to Plymouth. Along with Wall and Smith they formed an extremely potent spearhead. The season opened with an encouraging challenge match victory over Poole, now promoted to the Second Division. This was followed by home and away National Trophy success against

The 1952 Plymouth team.

Aldershot and an aggregate victory over Exeter which took Plymouth to the Southern League final where they defeated the Rayleigh Rockets. When the Second Division rounds started the Devils met Poole, who promptly ended Plymouth's winning run.

The Devils' successful run continued in the League and George Wall became the first visiting rider that season to score a maximum at Rayleigh, a feat he would repeat later in the year. By midseason Plymouth had climbed into second slot behind the leaders Wolverhampton. At this point John Deeley – previously in charge at Walthamstow – took over as team manager from Hazzard. This coincided with a decline in form for the Pennycross outfit who by August had slipped down to fourth place in the League table. Race night was now switched to Friday by popular demand, and then to add to Plymouth's problems Lansdale suddenly decided to quit. Although the Devils edged back up to second they had ridden more matches than their rivals and a crushing home defeat by eventual champions Rayleigh left them in a respectable third place.

In August an official Test match between England 'C' and Sweden attracted a crowd of almost 10,000. England started well and led by 10 points after ten races. Sweden fought back and quickly reduced the deficit in a bid to avoid their first defeat of the tour. Dan Forsberg and Olle Nygren overcame home favourites George Wall and Alan Smith to take maximum points from the final race and force a 54-54 draw. Smith topped the England score chart with 14 points, Wall scored 11 while Plymouth's other representative Pete Lansdale could only manage 4.

On the individual front Alan Smith made an unsuccessful challenge for Jack Unstead's Bronze Helmet in the spring but later in the year George Wall succeeded in relieving the Rayleigh rider of his title. The match race title soon returned to Essex as Wall lost it to Unstead's team mate Gerald Jackson.

As expected, Lansdale's retirement was short-lived and both he and Len Read were back at Pennycross in 1953 along with George Wall (who was unfortunately injured in a pre-season practice crash), Alan Smith, Bill Thatcher, Brian Hitchcock, Ted Stevens, Frank Wheeler and Doug Fursey. The season opened on Good Friday when Exeter's Goog Hoskin won the John A. Chapman Trophy with a 15-point maximum, while Ron Barrett equalled the track record.

In April Plymouth entertained Swedish touring side Filbyterna who won 66-42 with Svens Skoglund scoring an 18-point maximum and Ove Fundin 15. Alan Smith came closest to beating Skoglund and was the top Devil on 13.

Plymouth's League campaign began badly with a home defeat by Southampton. The Devils quickly made up for it by winning 52-32 away at near neighbours St Austell the following Tuesday. But the meeting was marred by tragedy when Plymouth's young Australian Ted Stevens died following a crash in heat 7. Stevens was in fourth place and could not avoid hitting the machines of Ken Monk and Jack Gates who had fallen ahead of him. He was flung into the fence and died in the ambulance on the way to hospital.

A minute's silence was observed for Stevens at Pennycross prior to the Devils' 49-35 League victory over Cardiff. Oxford forced a 54-54 draw and then Exeter won 43-41 at Pennycross. Even more amazingly St Austell, who had never ever won away from home since joining the Third Division in 1950, crossed the Tamar on Thursday 8 May and won 47-37 despite Devils' Alan Smith scoring a maximum.

Plymouth were dealt a second major blow when Thatcher suffered a fractured skull while racing at Southampton, and shortly afterwards Wall was forced to retire on medical grounds as a consequence of his crash earlier in the season. Indeed it was another season to forget for the Devils who subsequently finished bottom of the League.

The 1954 season was short-lived due to a further rapid decline in support at Pennycross. Yet another promoting company had taken over, headed by R.C. Byng and R.W. Prichard Jones. Major C.D. Gray MC was named as promoter and clerk of the course, while George Wall made a comeback contrary to medical advice.

Bill Thatcher.

The 1954 Plymouth team.

The Devils started with an away Southern Shield defeat at Exeter. Four days later on Good Friday a challenge match against Second Division Ipswich at Pennycross also resulted in a defeat for the Devils. The 45-39 scoreline could well have been closer had George Wall not crashed out in his opening ride.

Plymouth's interest in the National Trophy was again brief. The Devils were thrashed 69-38 in the first leg at Poole and then humiliated 63-43 by the Pirates back at Pennycross. The Devils claimed their first Southern Shield victory when they beat Exeter 43-41 on 6 May. The Falcons gained full revenge by rattling up 80 points against Plymouth in the Devon Derby at the County Ground two weeks later. If that was not bad enough Exeter followed up with a 76-32 win in the second leg at Pennycross to complete a 156-59 rout.

The situation was now becoming increasingly grim. Admission prices were increased and the programme carried a full breakdown of race-night expenses which totalled £439. Swindon were the final team to complete a Southern Shield double, before the Devils achieved a 49-36 success over Southampton in their first and what would turn out to be their last home National League match. Two days later the Devils rode their final away match at Coventry where they lost 54-30.

The Leicester Hunters were due at Pennycross in the League on Thursday 1 July but the rain again set in and the match was cancelled. At the same time came the announcement that Plymouth Speedway would close following the World Championship qualifying round on 8 July. Brian McKeown won the round by with 15 points, with Bob Roger on 14 and Malcolm Craven on 13.

In his programme notes that night team manager Don Weekes explained that the management needed 4,500 regular supporters to break even. The average gate in 1954 was 3,500 and the losses could no longer be sustained. The following week stock car racing arrived at Pennycross and attracted huge crowds, frequently double those that had turned up for speedway.

After a five-year break speedway returned to Plymouth on Good Friday (29 March) 1959. It returned under the Western Promotions banner of Trevor Redmond who had successfully run open-licence racing at St Austell the previous summer. The stadium owners were keen to see Pennycross used as much as possible and apart from the speedway, boxing and wrestling were also introduced under the management of Jack Burns and Dale Martin respectively.

The opening meeting attracted a bumper 10,000 crowd who saw Plymouth lose narrowly to a Midlands select by 49-47. Programmes from these meetings are very rare but show that the home side was nicknamed the Drakes and wore race jackets with a duck's head emblem. Split Waterman, scoring 10 points, led the team which also included Dick Harris, Ray Cresp, Norman Strachan, and former Devils Alan Smith and Pete Lansdale, with Francis Cann as reserve. The Midlands comprised Les McGillivray, Terry Small, Jack Unstead, Eric Hockaday, Jack Biggs, and Ronnie Ralph. Biggs top-scored with 13.

A West of England match race also took place in which Lansdale beat Trevor Redmond 2-0, and for an added bonus 500 Easter eggs were given away to the children during the afternoon while some fans also received newly introduced Premium Bonds.

The second meeting, the British League Pairs, took place on 23 April and was won by the Wimbledon duo of Ronnie Moore (15) and Bob Andrews (4). Second were Ian Williams and Mike Broadbanks representing Swindon while Plymouth's Alan Smith and Neil Street finished third. In the second half St Austell beat Exeter and Plymouth in the junior pairs. The crowd was down to 5,000 for this meeting but that would prove to be the average attendance for the rest of the season.

On Friday 15 May Plymouth, led by former world champion Peter Craven, beat Oxford 54-42. Craven scored a 15-point maximum and was supported by the Swindon trio of Neil Street (12), George White (11) and Mike Broadbanks (10). The Dane Arne Pander top scored for the Cheetahs with 11. A planned match between Plymouth and Poole on 25 June was cancelled due to a printers' strike which prevented the promoters from advertising the event in the press. The next meeting on 7 July saw a Combined Stars line-up take on the Swedish Lions. The result was a 48-48 draw with Ove Fundin and Rune Sormander both scoring a 15-point maximums for the Swedes. Geoff Mardon replaced Ronnie Moore for the Combined Stars and was joint top scorer with Ken McKinlay on 10 points.

The limited 1959 season came to a close on 3 September when McKinlay's Lions scored a narrow 38-34 victory over Briggs' Overseas Stars in a twelve-heat match. McKinlay paved the way for his team's victory with 10 points while Barry Briggs' 14 and 13 for Ronnie Moore made up the bulk of the Overseas total. This meeting also included sidecars in which Cornwall's Roy Wedlake, Ivor Toms and Chris Julian competed, sports cars and the newly introduced karts, which were demonstrated by Moore and Neil Street.

In 1960 Bristol promoter Eric Salmon set out to reintroduce League racing at Plymouth. Although his plans failed to materialise permission was given to run a

Plymouth Sports' Stadium

PENNYCROSS

THURSDAY, 3rd SEPT., 1959

AT 7.45 P.M.

1959 SPEED SHOW

Official Souvenir Programme 1/-.

A 1959 programme cover.

Western Cup competition with Exeter and St Austell towards the end of the season, but only two meetings took place at Pennycross.

The first, a Western Cup match between Plymouth and Bristol, took place on Thursday 8 September. Plymouth was represented by riders from Poole's Provincial League side and the result was a 36-36 draw. A week later a qualifying round of the Provincial League Riders Championship, originally scheduled to take place at Yarmouth, was raced at Pennycross. It was won by Rayleigh's Eric Hockaday with a 15-point maximum, second was Harry Bastable of Cradley Heath with 14 and third was Bristol Bulldogs' Cliff Cox (9) who was destined to become Plymouth's skipper in 1961.

Plymouth also rode an away Western Cup match at Exeter on Monday 19 September which they lost 40-38. Although a return match against the Falcons was advertised to take place at Pennycross on 22 September, it never materialised.

Following the sale of Bristol's Knowle Park stadium for redevelopment, the Bulldogs' promoter Eric Salmon decided to move his operation to Plymouth and run the team in the popular new Provincial League. Hopes were high that Salmon would bring the nucleus of his successful 1960 Bristol team with him, but only Cliff Cox, Pat Flanagan, and a set of race jackets reached Plymouth hence in 1961 the team would be known as the Bulldogs.

The new Plymouth line-up would also include Australian ex-pools winner Jack Scott, on loan from Southampton, Coventry's Maurie Mattingley, and Ron Bagley from Ipswich as well as Cornishmen Chris Julian, Chris Blewett, Ivor Toms and Ray Wickett who had all started out at St Austell.

The 1961 Plymouth Bulldogs. From left to right: Chris Blewett, Frank Evans, Ray Wickett, Cliff Cox (on bike), Jack Scott, Pat Flanagan, Ron Bagley, Chris Julian.

A chaotic start to the new era saw Plymouth lose 40-33 at home to Poole in a challenge match. 'It was nightmare', acknowledged Salmon. Flanagan, Ernie Baker and Norman Strachan all failed to appear while several other riders arrived late. Then Poole's Alan Kidd and Toms were both injured in a fourth heat accident. Further crashes and mechanical failures meant that by the end of the evening there were hardly any serviceable machines left in the pits. Such was the situation that Bagley was even forced to take eight rides for the Bulldogs so became top scorer with 14 points.

Fortunately by the second meeting the Bulldogs had sorted themselves out sufficiently to beat their old rivals Exeter (now promoted by former Devils Wally Mawdsley and Pete Lansdale) 44-34 in the first Provincial League match. Jack Scott made his debut in this meeting and scored the first of several maximums.

Plymouth quickly gained revenge for that opening night defeat by beating the Pirates 40-38 when the Dorset outfit returned in the League on 21 April. From then on Plymouth would prove unbeatable at home.

A first away success was achieved at Sheffield where the Bulldogs won 52-44 in the Knockout Cup, but despite the growing on-track success it was clear that early attendance figures were disappointing. Rumours soon began to circulate that Salmon was losing money and an early closure could be on the cards. Just to add to the promoter's problems Cox had been injured. On the positive side Jack Scott was rapidly becoming the talk of the Provincial League thanks to a string of double-figure scores including maximums for the Bulldogs in their home wins over Stoke and Rayleigh. He also won the Plymouth World Championship qualifying round with an unbeaten 15 points.

Sheffield and Middlesbrough were both dismissed 47-31, while the Bulldogs only lost by a single point, 46-45, at Exeter in the first leg of the revived Devon Derby. Three days later Plymouth clinched the trophy with a 52-44 victory in the second leg. The Bulldogs also lost narrowly at top of the table Poole (40-38) but won convincingly 53-25 at Wolverhampton before scoring their second success at Sheffield. This time they beat the Tigers 41-37 in the League. Back at Pennycross, Newcastle, Wolverhampton, Edinburgh and Cradley were all defeated but Edinburgh ended the Bulldogs' Knockout Cup aspirations by winning 56-40 at Old Meadowbank. The League fixtures had all been completed by mid-August and, thanks to their fine home record and away wins at Sheffield and Wolverhampton, the Bulldogs finished runners-up to champions Poole, their highest ever League position.

The remainder of the season consisted of challenge matches including a second home and away clash with Exeter. Plymouth won the first leg 55-23 and then achieved a 39-39 draw at the County Ground. It ended on Friday 1 September with the depleted Bulldogs going down 43-35 to a strong Pick of the League Select which included Jimmy Squibb, Ross Gilbertson, Len Silver and Geoff Mudge. Jack Scott was given permission to miss what would have been his final match at Pennycross as he was preparing for the semi-final of the World Championship to be staged at Wembley the following evening. Scott had enjoyed a superb run in the World Championship and was the only Provincial League rider to get within five rides of the world final. Sadly he had a dreadful night at the Empire Stadium where he only scored 2 points after a fall and an engine failure.

In the last programme Salmon acknowledged that public support was finally being attracted back to Pennycross and predicted that speedway would continue although he would not be the promoter. In 1962 Salmon's successor would be the flamboyant Bernard Curtiss, a PR man who sported a Jimmy Edwards-style moustache and is believed to have been responsible for introducing Capstan, then one of the major cigarette companies, to speedway sponsorship.

Curtiss quickly rebuilt the team. He signed Jimmy Squibb, talked former Exeter and New Cross star Bert Roger out of retirement, and managed to retain the services of Chris Julian, Chris Blewett and Ivor Toms who may well have joined Trevor Redmond's new venture at Neath. With Cliff Cox and Maurie Mattingley, now signed on a full transfer, also staying on, Curtis had the basis of a very good team, backed up by Ray Wickett and George Summers. The new promoter also gave Plymouth back the traditional 'Devils' nickname and race jacket, decked his team out in smart red jerseys, returned to Thursday race nights and appointed former Wimbledon rider Len Glover as team manager.

The strength of the new line-up was immediately apparent. Reigning League champions Poole Pirates were beaten 40-38 in the opening challenge match. A week later the Devils dispatched a Swindon B team 43-34, highlights of this match being shown on Westward TV. Exeter (still reeling from the death of Jack Unstead in a track crash at Ipswich the previous week) were beaten 43-35 at Pennycross in the Southern Cup on Good Friday. Three days later, the Devils forced a 39-39 draw at the County Ground in the second leg on Easter Monday.

After beating newcomers Neath Dragons at Pennycross, the Plymouth team travelled to Edinburgh for their opening Provincial League match. On the afternoon, the Devils went down 45-32, but later the Plymouth promotion protested that Monarchs' Doug Templeton had ridden with an illegal tyre. The SCB upheld the protest and deducted Templeton's 10 points. This now gave Plymouth a narrow 39-38 victory. It was also claimed that Bert Roger received a point in heat 5, even though he had pulled up with a mechanical problem and was a non-finisher.

First Division Wimbledon sent a B team to Plymouth which won 44-34, but a week later the Devils claimed their first home PL points thanks to a 55-22 victory over Wolverhampton. The following Sunday, Plymouth rode a challenge match at non-League Eastbourne where the Devils won 52-26. Stoke Potters visited Pennycross and were beaten 53-22, but the following evening turned the tables to win 41-36 back in the Potteries. Next the Devils visited the fellow Thursday track Sheffield and lost 54-23 to the Tigers, but 24 hours later in the return at Pennycross won 42-36.

Jimmy Squibb won the Plymouth World Championship Qualifying round on 7 June with 14 points, finishing ahead of Peter Jarman (13) and Ross Gilbertson (12). Earlier in the week Devils' skipper Cliff Cox had won the Exeter round with a 15-point maximum. A week later, on Whit Monday, Cox scored another 15 points, this time against the Falcons in the first leg of the Devon Rose Bowl at Pennycross which the Devils won 55-41.

The following Thursday the Devils could only manage a 39-39 draw against hard-charging Neath in the Provincial League. Cox notched another 12-point maximum, while Squibb scored 11 points, but the rest of the team provided poor support. Cox's

Chris Julian and Chris Blewett.

The 1962 Plymouth Devils. From left to right, back row: Maurie Mattingly, Cliff Cox, Bernard Curtiss, Jimmy Squibb, Chris Julian, Ivor Toms. Front row: Len Glover, Bert Roger, Chris Blewett.

unbeaten run came to an end at Exeter, where the Falcons won 44-34 and Len Silver ended Cliff's maximum hopes in the very last race. Sadly that week's meeting at Pennycross heralded the start of a terminal decline in the Devils' fortunes.

Rumours were again circulating that the speedway was on the verge of closure due to lack of support and matters did not improve when team manager Len Glover was publicly sacked during a best pairs meeting. Curtis had devised a complex formula for this meeting but unfortunately the programmes failed to arrive, which made it extremely difficult to organise. When things went drastically wrong Glover took the blame in full view of the fans. Ray Wickett was also put on the free transfer list after he had failed to warn Curtiss that he could not repair his bike in time for the meeting. To add to the problems, several heats were only contested by three riders and in some cases only two as Maurie Mattingley and Ivor Toms both withdrew after a spectacular crash in the third heat. The meeting was eventually won by Cox (13) and Alby Smith (5). Afterwards it was claimed that the programmes did not arrive from the London printers until 8am the next day. Perhaps significantly the following week's programme was published locally.

With Mattingley injured, the Devils only just managed to hold Edinburgh Monarchs to a draw in which Plymouth's task was not made any easier by Wayne Briggs, who scored a faultless maximum.

From then on Plymouth's chances of repeating their '61 success were minimal. Even though the Devils won all their remaining home matches, they failed to win away. The following week they managed to beat Leicester without Cox, Mattingley or Bert Roger, who had decided to end his comeback. Lew Philp was rapidly coming to prominence, but broke a bone in his leg at the beginning of August while riding a challenge match against St Austell.

Plymouth's qualifying round of the PLRC was cancelled due to rain and then the Devils went out of the Knockout Cup at the hands of the eventual winners, Exeter. The Falcons won the sudden-death match at the County Ground 53-43. The PLRC round was re-staged on 30 August and won by Jimmy Squibb after a run-off with Jon Erskine.

The Devils completed their Provincial League fixtures with a narrow 38-37 win against Newcastle. Chris Julian scored a maximum and Cox 11, but Squibb had an off night with just 3 points. The penulti-mate match, the West of England

Cliff Cox.

Championship, saw Plymouth (31) beat Poole (27) and Exeter (14). Cox and Squibb were unbeaten for the Devils, while Blewett happily walked away from a very spectacular crash.

The season ended, in superb fashion, with the Westward Television Champion of Champions Trophy. Although a number of riders were non-starters, the meeting was action-packed and at the end of the evening Devils Jimmy Squibb and Chris Blewett were tied on 14 points. Blewett had dropped his only point to Ross Gilbertson in heat 9 while Squibb missed out to Blewett. However the bearded Devil gained revenge by winning the run-off.

Cliff Cox and Jimmy Squibb had both qualified for the final of the Provincial League Riders Championship at Belle Vue where they finished well down the order with 5 and 6 points respectively. Sadly the earlier rumours proved correct and Plymouth duly closed down again during the winter, not because of poor performances, but again due to lack of support. It seemed that even with a winning team, not enough Plymouthians wanted to support the Devils.

The final era of speedway at Plymouth began in 1968 with the launch of the British League Division Two. The British League had proved a huge success since it was formed at the beginning of 1965 and as a result the promoters needed a source of new riders. A Second Division was seen at the way to develop new junior talent and League was launched in May 1968. Exeter promoters Wally Mawdsley and Pete Lansdale (both former Plymouth riders) decided to re-open two tracks, Plymouth and Weymouth, with Lansdale taking charge at Pennycross. They were joined in the Plymouth venture by local bookmaker Fred Osborn who held the stadium lease. The nucleus of the team would be Exeter juniors Mike Cake, Phil Woodcock, Tony George and Dave Whittaker. The veteran Falcon Eric Howe, whose career had been halted by a serious accident in 1963, was also given a team place but only made one appearance before being replaced by Chris Roynon.

By now the red shale track at Pennycross had been replaced with tarmac for the stock cars but the new promotion overcame this by laying a surface of silver sand on top of the asphalt.

The Devils' first match took place at Rayleigh where they lost 40-34 in an exciting contest on a very wet track. There was plenty of action with no fewer than fifteen falls in the thirteen heats. Heat 7 saw Tony George win a race of attrition 3-0 after Graeme Smith was excluded for unfair riding, Geoff Maloney suffered an engine failure and Cake fell off. Better fortune followed at Canterbury where the Devils were joint winners of a four-team tournament with Weymouth.

The opening match against Weymouth at Pennycross fell victim to a heavy shower at 6.20 p.m. The rain proved too much for the newly laid track which was already wet following a day of constant drizzle. The Eagles returned a week later and the Devils achieved their first win in front of an encouraging crowd of 3,000. Mike Cake and Phil Woodcock headed the Plymouth score chart with 9 points each, and would have claimed paid maximums but for falls. Tony George showed great determination by dragging his bike across the finish line by its front wheel to claim second place in heat 9. He had been leading the race when he fell and was narrowly missed by Cake.

Weymouth's Roy Carter and Chris Yeatman were not so lucky and crashed into the fence. George, however, picked himself up and pulled his bike a quarter of a lap to the flag. The track surface caused problems as, with nothing to bind it, the sand tended to drift off the racing line out to the fence, but this would later be rectified.

Having gained their first League points, the Devils remained unbeaten at home with top men Mike Cake and Chris Bass virtually unstoppable at Pennycross. Bass, a 28-year-old Australian, made his debut against Nelson Admirals on 21 June with 11 points as Plymouth won 50-28. Unfortunately he would only ride nine further matches thanks to a broken collarbone.

Plymouth eventually finished fourth in the inaugural Second Division championship thanks to a single away win at Berwick, and but for defeats in their final away matches at Canterbury and Crayford may well have finished as runners-up. The weather also hindered efforts to re-establish Plymouth Speedway as of the nineteen meetings staged at Pennycross that summer five were rained off, including the first and last, while several more were run in adverse conditions, especially that against Berwick in which the last three races took place in a thunderstorm.

Mike Cake's supremacy was highlighted by his success in two individual events. He won the Guards Trophy with 14 points, and the Bromley Bowl with a maximum. Cake was prevented from achieving a hat-trick by Bass who won the final of the twelve-heat speedway section of the August bank holiday Cavalcade of Speed.

The object of reopening Pennycross had always been to develop riders for parent track Exeter and in this regard the venture was an undoubted success. Cake, Woodcock, Bass and George all made progress and both Cake and Woodcock enjoyed reasonable success at the top level. But Plymouth's greatest find would be Exeter based Bob Coles. Coles had started out earlier in the year in second halves at the County Ground where he constantly pestered Lansdale for an opportunity at Pennycross. After several refusals he was eventually given a chance when other riders failed to turn up. Bob impressed sufficiently to be given a chance in the team against Crayford when Woodcock injured his shoulder and Ian Gills' machine had been written off in a car crash. He scored 5 points against the Highwaymen and there after was an ever present for the Devils.

The Exeter promoters pulled out in 1969 leaving Fred Osborn to run Plymouth alone. At that time First Division tracks had first claim on their riders which frequently meant the Second Division team going into action without their heat leaders. Osborn was determined that this would no longer happen at Plymouth, and refused to sign First Division riders on loan thus the Devils lost the bulk of their successful 1968 team as Cake, Woodcock, Bass, and George did not return. Dave Whitaker took over the captaincy while Chris Roynon and Keith Marks stayed on along with Bob Coles who so far had only ridden three matches for the Devils. Former Devil Ray Wickett appeared at the pre-season practice but was not seen again. Osborn meanwhile signed Adrian Degan, who failed to score in two home matches before disappearing and John Ellis, a veteran of West Country second half races. Ellis made six appearances for the Devils before being injured. Much more successful was an unknown youngster called Colin Sanders, a garage mechanic from Bristol, who amazingly scored 11 points in his first match, a home win over Ipswich in May.

PLYMOUTH SPEEDWAY

PLYMOUTH versus WEYMOUTH

24th MAY, 1968, at 7.30 p.m.

Official Programme 1/-

A 1968 programme cover.

The season got underway with a challenge match against Eastbourne which the Devils won 41-37. The match also saw 16-year-old Dave Jessup make his debut for the Eagles.

Plymouth went on to win nine home matches, the same as the previous year, but also lost six times in front of their own fans. The Devils also subsequently failed to win away from home and finished one place above bottom club King's Lynn II whose season had also failed to live up to expectations after recording an early win at Pennycross.

By mid-season the growing number of defeats was being reflected in declining attendance figures so in a bid to boost flagging support Osborn talked former Devils' favourite Cliff Cox into making a comeback. The promoter also went to Reading in place of the team manager George Newton and returned with two new riders, John Hammond and Stuart Wallace. Hammond would ride twenty-two matches for the Devils but Wallace only made a single appearance.

Colin Sanders continued to make outstanding progress. He scored 11 points away at Crayford, more than half the Plymouth total as the Devils were defeated 56-21. Back at Pennycross he rattled off 12-point maximums against Nelson and Rayleigh. Cox made his eagerly awaited comeback against the Rockets but failed to score. In an effort to rebuild his confidence Osborn restricted the former Plymouth skipper to appearances in home matches only. Ex-pop singer and Newport junior Ian Terrar was given a second-half trial while Australian Paul Sly made a couple of appearances as Osborn attempted to strengthen his side.

In July Eastbourne snatched a 40-38 victory at Pennycross thanks to a last heat 5-1. Plymouth appeared to have the race under control but Dave Whitaker lost control while leading and took out his partner Chris Roynon, who was too bruised to continue. Cox replaced him in the rerun and was holding down a match-winning second place behind Dave Jessup when his engine let go.

A week later Berwick Bandits won 44-34 after Sanders walked out following a dispute with Osborn in the pits after falling twice in one of his races and being excluded from the rerun. The matter was eventually cleared up and Sanders stayed at Plymouth. On 1 August he teamed up with Clark Facey to win the Pussycat Club Pairs.

The Devils won their remaining home British League fixtures, beating Canterbury (40-38), Long Eaton (51-27) and Reading (42-36) and also defeated Exeter B and Dorset in a three-team tournament.

The match against Reading Racers on 29 August would prove to be the final League match staged at Pennycross. Bob Coles was the Devils top scorer with 11 points, but the honour of winning the last race went to Reading's Mike Vernam. The Plymouth season eventually ended in early October when Coles stormed through his heats, semi and the final to win the Bromley Bowl.

During the winter Osborn planned to run regular training schools and also rip up the tarmac stock car track which would enable him to rebuild the speedway track. But in March 1970 he announced that he had sold Plymouth's British League licence to newcomers Peterborough and would in future only be staging open-licence racing at Pennycross. This, he claimed, would allow him to build up both the team and the following for a League return in 1971 at a 'different' venue. Sadly this idea never materialised.

The stadium at Pennycross had been purchased by Plymouth City Council in 1962 for £41,000 with the intention of building a new Sutton High School on the site. That plan had not materialised either and in the meantime the stadium had become more and more dilapidated. However Fred Osborn kept his promise regarding the track and, with the stock cars gone, replaced the tarmac with shale. Devils' rider Chris Roynon, a JCB driver by trade, did the work, tearing up 600 tons of asphalt and relaying the 413-yard track with shale. Times would certainly be quicker but not the 10-second difference that Osborn had predicted.

The 1970 season began with a challenge match against Eastbourne on Good Friday, 27 March. The Plymouth team consisted of Mike Vernam, John Hammond, Bob Coles, Graham Wheeler, Chris Roynon, Clark Facey, and local boy Malcolm Evely. Despite a 15-point maximum from Vernam the Eagles edged ahead thanks to a 5-1 in heat 8 after which the Devils were never quite able to get back on terms. Coles won his first three races but missed out on his maximum when he finished third in the final race.

After this meeting the council withdrew permission for speedway to take place at Pennycross. It appeared that the Devils were finished but then it became apparent that the site had been leased to a local businessman, John Weight. Fred Osborn's initial negotiations were unsuccessful but eventually after six weeks his offer was accepted and the bikes returned to Pennycross for the last time.

Between 10 April and 10 July the Devils raced nine challenge matches. They beat Romford twice, newly formed Peterborough Panthers, Swindon 'B', Rayleigh, Crewe and Newport 'B' but lost to Reading and Eastbourne. Sadly crowds were virtually non-existent with the predictable result that on Thursday 17 July speedway finally came to an end at Plymouth. The last meeting was an individual event for the Bromley Bowl which was won by Eastbourne's Mac Woolford after a run off with Colin Sanders after both had finished on 14 points. Bob Coles was third with 13.

Greyhound racing continued at Pennycross until the following year after which the stadium was torn down and replaced with industrial units. Efforts to find an alternative site have been made by various would-be promoters including Exeter's Colin Hill but so far none have been forthcoming.

PART III

ST AUSTELL

ST AUSTELL

It is not possible to go much further South West than Cornwall and as such it is a very long way from the major centres of motor sport. Probably because of its distant location the Duchy has always been a hotbed for all kinds of motorcycling and in the fifties even staged events for Formula One racing cars on an airfield circuit at Davidstowe.

Prior to the Second World War regular grass-track racing events were held at Rocky Park by the St Austell Motor Club which attracted huge crowds. Many top speedway riders travelled down to Cornwall to compete in these meetings, among them Jack Parker, Bill Kitchen, and Pete Lansdale. The popularity of grass-track continued after the war, and consequently it was decided to create a purpose-built speedway stadium. The idea was the brainchild of Mr J. Luke who enlisted the aid of A.D. 'Chirpy' Richards. Together they formed a company and decided to build their new speedway stadium on a 14-acre site at Par Moor on the outskirts of St Austell not far from the sea. The new stadium was described as the 'Wembley of the West' by the *Western Morning News*, which noted that although the venue so far lacked covered accommodation for the public, this was planned for later. It was also intended that the new stadium would be used for other sports including football, cycling, athletics, gymkhanas and band contests. The project was financed by the Luke family, while advice on the design of the track was given by Jack Parker, Bill Kitchen and Vic Duggan. The track itself measured 360 yards, was surfaced with crushed local granite and opened on Tuesday 14 June 1949.

Although the stadium opened too late for St Austell to be accepted as members in the National League that season, permission was given by the Speedway Control Board for the track to stage open-licence meetings. This was an immediate success with a crowd of 12,000 flocking to see Peter Robinson's Select beat Cyril Quick Select 46-37 on the opening night. Considering that at the time the entire population of St Austell was only 8,000 and petrol was still rationed, this truly was a remarkable achievement. The SCB had also given permission for two senior riders to race in each meeting, so that summer the world's top speedway stars were regularly seen in Cornwall. On opening night Robinson's side even included two Cornish riders, Des Tamlyn and Adrian Kessell, who amazingly continues to race regularly in present-day grass-track events.

The next two meetings saw a West of England team first lose to Poole, then beat Tamworth. The newly formed Oxford Cheetahs were the next side to visit the Cornish stadium, and clinched a 43-41 victory over the Mick Mitchell Select in the final heat. Mitchell's spectacular leg-trailing style quickly endeared him to the Cornish fans. The Hull Angels skipper won the second-half final and soon became a big favourite at Par Moor.

The first time a team representing St Austell was seen in action at the Cornish Stadium was on 12 July when the 'Badgers' were defeated 46-34 by West Country neighbours Exeter Falcons. The Badgers line-up included Mick Mitchell, who scored a 12

91

ST.AUSTELL SPEEDWAY

OFFICIAL PROGRAMME 6d.

BADGERS v. EXETER FALCONS

Tuesday, 12th July, 1949, 7.15

A 1949 programme cover.

point maximum, Adrian Kessell, George Craig, Des Tamblyn, Alan Chambers, Ticker James, Cecil Macey, and Ken Blair.

A week later St Austell had become the Gulls, and the nickname, which would last for the next fifty years, was used for the first time when Poole Pirates returned to the Cornish Stadium and maintained their winning run at the new track.

At the beginning of August Jack Parker, then England's greatest rider, travelled to Cornwall to officially switch on the new floodlights. Crowds of 10,000 would be commonplace that summer. Among the other attractions were a Leg Trailers Night, and a clash between teams led by two younger Australian stars, Graham Warren and Jack Biggs. The action that night got off to a controversial start when, after a neck-and-neck first race, Biggs pipped Warren on the line and both were credited with equalling the track record. However the referee expressed himself doubtful about the start and ordered a rerun. Biggs won again and this time broke the record with a time of 68.25 seconds. Warren, who was not beaten again, later reduced the record to 68.0 seconds.

Early in September Cornwall's top speedway rider, Bruce Semmens, rode at Par Moor for the first time and was given a tremendous reception by the local fans even though his team was beaten 50-34 by George Newton's select. The Black Prince, Arthur Forrest, was also a regular competitor, and among the other top riders to appear that season were Vic and Ray Duggan, Norman Parker, Mike Erskine, Oliver Hart and Wilbur Lamoureaux.

By mid-October the crowds were still flocking in but the weather was making itself felt. An unofficial international between England and Australia scheduled for Tuesday 19 October was postponed for 24 hours due to rain. When the match eventually went ahead the Lions defeated the Kangaroos 44-39. Cyril Roger of New Cross was top Lion with 12 points and inflicted the only defeat of the evening on Kangaroos' skipper Jack Biggs who in turn equalled the track record. The season continued to the end of the month and climaxed with a gala match between teams led by the newly crowned world champion Tommy Price and Lloyd Goffe.

After the success of their open-licence season the St Austell management had little difficulty getting their team accepted by the Third Division of the National League for 1950. By now the public had become used to seeing the top riders in action at the Cornish Stadium so manager Chirpy Richards faced the tough task of putting together an entertaining and competitive side which would retain that interest. Sadly he failed to attract any real star men, due in the main to Cornwall's far flung location, and was forced to put out an under-strength team which lost its first fifteen League matches.

The second season opened at Cornish Stadium with the Silver Rose Bowl, a pairs meeting won by Mick Mitchell and George Gower. A week later the Gulls achieved their first victory beating Exeter 43-41 in a challenge match. The initial St Austell line-up included Norman Street, a former Hastings Saxon who was the nephew of Vic Duggan, Maurie McDermott, Alf Viccary, George Gower, Larry Young, Ken James, Rusty Wainwright and Broncho Slade. Crowd favourite Mick Mitchell had promised that if Hull did not run he would like to ride for St Austell. When Hull closed he asked for a move to Cornwall but his request was refused by the Speedway Control Board. Mitchell appealed against the decision but lost when it went to arbitration.

The National League action commenced with a 53-30 home defeat by Poole, which instantly highlighted the Gulls' weaknesses, and veteran Broncho Slade was speedily replaced by an up-and-coming Aussie, Peter Moore. A week later Aldershot won 48-35 at Cornish Stadium then Tamworth won twice, in both the League and the National Trophy. Three more home defeats followed, Oxford 47-37, Leicester 50-34 and Swindon 44-39 before a 52-32 victory was achieved over the Liverpool Chads. Chirpy Richards claimed that the change of luck came about as the result of his being dive-bombed by a seagull at Mevagissey on the afternoon of the match.

Harold Bull was signed from Walthamstow, Ray Ellis joined from New Cross, and a Pole, Max Rech also arrived to boost the Gulls who now began to win more regularly. Exeter were defeated 52-31, and Poole 45-39 in a match which attracted the biggest crowd of the season. A week later Rayleigh were thrashed 60-24, and then St Austell achieved their highest score when Swindon were humiliated 68-16. Oxford drew 42-42 before the Gulls rattled up another 60-plus tally against Rayleigh. Liverpool however sprang a late season surprise by returning to Par Moor and claiming a 52-32 win in the Gulls' penultimate home match.

Away from home it was strictly one way traffic with the only close result coming at Liverpool where the Gulls narrowly missed out 42-41. As a consequence of all those home defeats St Austell finished bottom of the League table.

Mick Mitchell finally got his wish and joined the Gulls from Leicester for the 1951 season. Ray Ellis was transferred to Swindon and Maurie McDermott also left. Norman Street, Harold Bull and Ken James were all retained, and Allan Quinn was signed on loan from Harringay. Ticker James came from Poole to join Ken Monk, Max Rech and the promising Maurice Hutchens.

The season opened on Tuesday 24 April with a challenge match against Plymouth who had returned to the Third Division. The move gave the Gulls a genuine local derby which St Austell won narrowly 43-41. A second challenge match against Aldershot was halted after eight heats with the Gulls leading 27-20 thanks to driving rain having turned the track in a quagmire. The following week the Gulls raced their first League match, losing 48-36 to Exeter. Having also lost away at Poole, St Austell collected their first points when they overcame League newcomers Cardiff Dragons 43-41 at Par Moor in a last-heat decider.

Plymouth inflicted the Gulls' second home defeat at the end of May, but June started well with a 50-34 win over Swindon. A week later Poole won 56-28 in what would be St Austell's biggest home defeat of the season. The Gulls now rattled up wins over Aldershot, Cardiff, Long Eaton, Rayleigh and Swindon. Plymouth were also defeated 50-34 in a challenge match at the start of July but the following week veteran Mick Mitchell, who had struggled all season to find his old form, crashed into the fence and was taken to hospital with serious concussion. He did not ride again that summer. The Gulls' run of seven successive home wins ended abruptly when Poole won for the second time in Cornwall, this time by 53-26. Undeterred, St Austell won four more home League fixtures including a tight 43-41 victory over Exeter, before missing out to Plymouth in the final match. Away from home it was the same old story. The Gulls suffered their worst beating at Cardiff where they went down 66-18, but were actually leading 11-7 at

Poole when the match was halted by rain with both Street and Bull having won races. Despite the continued poor away form, St Austell managed to climb off the bottom of the table, finishing above Long Eaton and Wolverhampton in eighth place.

The USA touring team proved a huge attraction when they visited Cornwall in August. Their visit attracted a huge crowd who witnessed a tremendous battle, which ended in a 42-42 draw. The track record also took a hammering. It was broken twice during the evening and the new record, 67.4 seconds, was eventually shared by Allan Quinn and American No.1 Ernie Roccio. The Americans were quickly booked for a return visit and flew in again from their base in Dublin later in the month this time to race Cornwall. Second time around, the home side were just too strong for the American Eagles and won 45-39. Roccio again broke the track record, reducing it to 67.0 seconds.

The 1952 season opened with a 50-34 win over Aldershot. The Third Division had now been renamed the Southern League and the Gulls team was Ken James, Norman Street, Allan Quinn, Ticker James, Harold Bull, Mick Mitchell, Maurice Hutchens and Max Rech. Quinn scored a maximum and Mitchell was only beaten by Basil Harris. Exeter won the opening Southern League match 55-29 at Par Moor, but Quinn scored his second maximum as Swindon were defeated the following week. Two more League points were gained with a victory over Long Eaton but those points were subsequently deducted when the Archers prematurely withdrew from the League. Quinn again made his mark by equalling the track record, which was already jointly held by Bill Holden, Bill Kitchen and Ernie Roccio. The Gulls lost at Exeter but won at home to Plymouth.

It was at this point that Mr Luke gave up his interest in the Gulls. The new promoters were C.J.C. Selleck and R.P. Jones, who engaged well-known frame-maker Vic Kermond as team manager. Ken Monk returned to the team after a long lay-off in place of the veteran Mick Mitchell, who was finding points hard to come by on the slicker shale tracks that had replaced the deep cinder surfaces, while Jimmy Gleed and Ray Thackwell came in at reserve. The Gulls scored a 1-point victory over Aldershot, whose Ivor Powell clocked a time of 66.0 seconds in the first race, one whole second under the track record.

The Gulls went down to a shock 54-30 defeat to Ipswich, in what had been expected to be an easy win for the Cornish outfit, followed by a further setback when Maurice Hutchens and the James brothers, Ticker and Ken, all decided to retire, leaving a big hole in the side. To fill the gap Johnny Bradford, who had ridden seventeen matches for the Gulls the previous year, returned along with new Aussie hopeful Gordon Leigh. A couple of ex-First Division men, Lloyd Goffe and Dick Harris also arrived on the scene in Cornwall. The away struggle continued but home wins were recorded over Southampton, eventual League champions Rayleigh, and Swindon. George Newton arrived to live in Cornwall and soon became involved at the St Austell track. George made his debut for the Gulls in a home defeat against Plymouth at Par Moor but won his first race. Around this time Harris and Rech were injured and unfortunately it was not long before Newton joined them.

St Austell staged an England 'C' *v.* Sweden test match on Friday 22 July, attracting a crowd of 11,000 to the Cornish Stadium. Gulls' Norman Street was given the honour of

ST. AUSTELL
SPEEDWAY

THE GULLS
OF
ST. AUSTELL

Versus

PLYMOUTH

GREAT SOUTHERN LEAGUE
AND LOCAL DERBY MATCH

TUESDAY, JULY 15th, 1952, at 7.45 p.m.

OFFICIAL PROGRAMME **6**D.

A 1952 programme cover.

being named as captain of England but had a disappointing night scoring just 4 points. The Swedes totally dominated the meeting, as they had done the series, winning 65-42 with a superb display of sharp gating and white line riding. Rune Sormander swept to an 18-point maximum while former Gull Maurie McDermott, who stepped in at the last minute, was England's solitary race winner in heat 2. This also proved to be the home nation's only heat advantage as Pete Lansdale finished third for a 4-2, before becoming England's leading scorer with 11.

Back on the domestic front Exeter completed the double by winning 43-41 at Par Moor after hammering the Gulls 52-31 at the County Ground the previous week. Nevertheless St Austell bounced back in remarkable style to defeat League leaders Rayleigh Rockets 43-40 at Par Moor. This was no mean achievement by the struggling Gulls. Meanwhile the casualty list continued to grow. Ken Monk fractured his shoulder blade and several ribs, Harris damaged an arm and a shoulder, while Norman Street was

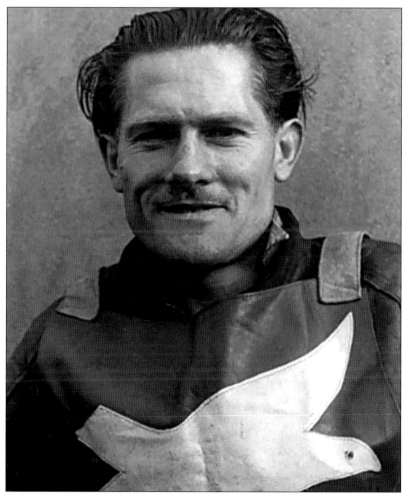

George Newton.

advised to rest by his doctor after racing ten meetings in two weeks during which time he covered more than 3,500 miles on non-motorway roads.

Aston Quinn was signed from Southampton, followed by Charlie Hayden, Derek Timms and the extraordinarily nicknamed 'Bambi' Royle coming in to bolster the flagging Gulls. The seemingly endless away defeats continued, while at home St Austell also lost to Cardiff, Ipswich and Wolverhampton, and not even a moral boosting victory over fellow strugglers Southampton, could save the Gulls from another wooden spoon.

On Tuesday 16 September St Austell beat Aldershot but the celebrations were marred when a helicopter crashed on the Cornish Stadium during the interval. The helicopter, which was taking part in a Battle of Britain display, was attempting to land on the centre green. Fifty feet from the ground it went out of control and narrowly missed the referee's box before crashing into the car park, killing the pilot and an unfortunate spectator who was attending his first speedway meeting.

The season ended with a nine-heat match against Bradford in which George Newton made his final racing appearance as a rider. In 1953 he would take over as team manager. His first season got underway with a 56-28 defeat at Exeter on Monday 13 April, and it was immediately clear that it would be the same old story on the road. Efforts had again been made to improve the Gulls' results by bringing in new blood. Alf Webster, former Exeter Falcon Johnnie Sargeant, Jackie Gates, Dennis Newton, on loan from Wembley, and Cyril Maidment would all make their debuts for St Austell as well as a host of New Zealanders including Graham Williams, the Gulls' original undertaker, Maury McHugh and Kevin Bock.

Further defeats followed at Swindon (60-23) where Kevin Bock and Belle Vue junior Bob Duckworth replaced Norman Street and Ken Monk, and at home to Ipswich (44-40) which saw Graham Williams lose his team place to John Yates.

Plymouth's win at Par Moor was marred by the tragic death of their young Australian youngster Ted Stevens. St Austell had to wait until mid-May before notching their first Southern League victory, a 50-34 success against the Oxford Cheetahs. Then to the delight of their long-suffering fans the Gulls scored what would be their only away win of the season, and indeed of that era, when they defeated near neighbours Plymouth Devils 47-37 at Pennycross. They also completed their first-ever double when they beat the Devils by the same score back at Cornish Stadium.

Boosted by their success St Austell then beat Cardiff Dragons 46-38 but the result was expunged from the records when the Welsh track closed due to lack of support shortly afterwards. Swindon confidently arrived in Cornwall on 8 July having only lost four of their previous twelve matches and suffered a shock 47-37 defeat. Two days later the Gulls almost achieved a second away win before losing narrowly 43-41 at Ipswich.

By now St Austell were on something of a roll, so much so that title challenging Rayleigh Rockets were beaten 42-40 in a last-heat decider. The Gulls found themselves at the heart of the championship race again a week later when the other contenders Exeter Falcons arrived at Par Moor eager to win where rivals Rayleigh had failed. This time the scores stood at 39-39 going into the fourteenth and final race. Sadly for Cornish hopes Monk and Gates could not match the speed of Goog Hoskin and Jack Geran from the tapes. Subsequently the Falcons snatched a 5-1 and the match.

ST. AUSTELL

SPEEDWAY

GRAND CHALLENGE MATCH AND LOCAL DERBY

Cornish 'Gulls' v. Plymouth 'Devils'

Tuesday, 28th July, at 7.45 .m.

OFFICIAL PROGRAMME 9d.

A 1953 programme cover.

Swindon were beaten again, this time 61-23 with Webster, Monk, Bull and Gates all scoring maximums. By now the Gulls had gained another New Zealander, Bryce Subritsky, but once more things started to go wrong for St Austell. With Street out for another long spell due to family commitments, McHugh not yet experienced enough to hold down a heat leader slot, Subritsky injured, Bock taking several knocks and Yates retiring, the team, not surprisingly, lost a lot of its winning power.

Defeats at Southampton, Swindon, Ipswich, Rayleigh, Plymouth and Exeter coupled with home losses at the hands of the Saints, Witches and Rockets added up to nine successive matches without a win. The situation had reached rock bottom and Gulls general manager 'Chirpy' Richards made no excuses pointing to badly prepared equipment as the root cause of the problem. He also had the courage to write in the St Austell programme that 'it was the duty of the team, to the supporters, the management and to the other promoters to "put first things first" and ensure that they gave full value for the money they were being paid'.

St Austell's rout was halted at the end of August when the Gulls beat Oxford 47-37. However the Gulls still had one last part to play in the battle for the League championship when they defeated Exeter 43-40 at Cornish Stadium on 8 September, but it still did not prevent the Falcons from winning the title, albeit after a great deal of argument. St Austell's final home League win came against Southampton who, like so many other teams, exacted full revenge by winning 63-21 when the Gulls round off their fixtures at Banister Court.

Another season of poor results left the Gulls seventh in the League table, one place above bottom team Plymouth. It was the end of the road for League racing in Cornwall as the SCB refused to renew the Gulls' licence in January 1954.

The new craze for stock car racing soon spread to St Austell where it was introduced at the Cornish Stadium by New Zealand speedway international Trevor Redmond and his father-in-law and former Aldershot promoter Bob Elcott. Four years later in 1958 this duo applied to stage open-licence speedway during the peak holiday months. Their application was successful and the first meeting in July was the West of England Open, won by Jack Geran from Neil Street and Alf Hagon. Jack remembers that TR gave him a bogus cheque for £3,000 carefully

Trevor Redmond.

signed in the name of Charlie Knott, the Southampton promoter. Never one to miss an opportunity Redmond spotted a member of the public filming the racing with a ciné camera and claimed that he was a Hollywood producer preparing a speedway film.

The first team matches saw St Austell lose 54-42 to Swindon but in the next the Gulls led by legendary Swedish world champion Ove Fundin beat Poole 34-26. The world's top stars had once again become regular visitors to the Cornish Stadium and the short season ended with an International Pairs meeting, which was won Peter Craven and Ken McKinlay from Barry Briggs and former St Austell rider Bob Duckworth. Briggs went on to win Champion of Champions individual second-half event.

Redmond was quick to realise that the peak holiday months between July and September were the most beneficial to stage speedway in Cornwall. In the late fifties British speedway was at its lowest ebb and, with only a handful of League teams operating, riders were more than happy to accept open bookings despite the amount of travelling involved. The 1959 season opened with Australia's Peter Moore, a one time Gull winning the Stars of the West Trophy. In a three-team tournament the following week St Austell beat Exeter and Bristol. An unofficial international between the Lions and the Kiwis resulted in a 46-44 win for the home team. The Gulls were then beaten 56-34 by a London Select while Swindon's Tep Teodorwicz top-scored for the Continentals in their 3TT victory over the Lions led by Peter Craven and the Australians. Jack Geran and Neil Street teamed up to win the 50 Guineas Trophy pairs event and a week later St Austell beat Wimbledon and Poole in another three-team match before the Stars ended the season on Tuesday 2 September by beating the Lions 40-32.

The 1960 season followed a similar pattern with St Austell racing a series of challenge matches against fledgling Provincial League teams Rayleigh, Cradley Heath, Poole and Bristol. The Gulls won all of these plus a match against the Midlands Stars, although Bristol forced a draw. St Austell's only defeat came against a side billed simply as 'The Stars' who won 34-32. Redmond himself had teamed up with Chris Julian from Fraddon to win the opening night Best Pairs.

The Gulls also rode two away matches. They finished second behind the Bulldogs at Bristol in a four-team tournament that also included Yarmouth and Poole, and lost 45-27 in a late season challenge at Exeter.

Wolverhampton, Exeter, Plymouth, Ipswich and Poole all rode challenge matches at Par Moor in 1961. The opening event, the aptly named Stars and Stripes Trophy on 4 July, was won by the Poole duo of Geoff Mudge and Alan Kidd, while a crowd of 4,500 saw Mudge, now partnering Brian Brett, win the Cornish Championship. Martin Ashby won the top individual prize after a run-off with Redmond. The season's third pairs meeting, the Capstan Trophy, at the end of August was won by the Plymouth pairing of Maurie Mattingley and Cliff Cox.

The following year, 1962, Trevor Redmond attempted to reintroduce speedway to Wales. His choice of venue was Neath's Abbey Stadium. Alas difficulties began to surface even before the new track opened. It was a very wet spring and the stadium lacked adequate shelter, and just to add to TR's problems his first meeting coincided with the outbreak of a smallpox epidemic in Neath during which the public were discouraged from congregating in large crowds. Subsequently the venture failed and permission was

Francis Cann pursues the Poole Pirates at the Cornish Stadium.

granted by the Speedway Control Board for several of the Welsh Dragons' Provincial League matches to be staged at St Austell.

The Cornish season opened on Tuesday 3 July with the Inter Town Trophy won by Wayne Briggs and Francis Cann representing Liskeard. The first Provincial League match on 10 July saw St Austell/Neath beat Edinburgh Monarchs 42-36. A week later the combined Gulls/Dragons beat Stoke 50-28. The next match was a challenge against Exeter which resulted in a 39-39 draw, followed a week later by another Provincial League match in which Bradford were beaten 51-27.

August saw St Austell defeat near neighbours Plymouth Devils 40-35 in a challenge match. This local derby not surprisingly attracted the best crowd of the season, an attendance of more than 4,000, but a League match against Newcastle the following week was rained off.

On 21 August Neath's Provincial Riders Championship qualifying round was staged at the Cornish Stadium. It was won by Plymouth skipper Cliff Cox with a 15-point maximum from the Gulls' Trevor Redmond, Glyn Chandler and Charlie Monk who all finished on 12 points. The penultimate meeting, a three-team tournament, was won by Cornwall (26) from the Midlands (24) and Wales (22).

The campaign ended on 5 September with the restaged match against Newcastle Diamonds. St Austell/Neath won 44-34 to complete an unbeaten home run at the Cornish Stadium. The Neath/St Austell team finished second to Poole in the Provincial League championship, ahead of third-placed Exeter.

★★★★★★★★★★★★★★★★★★★★★★★★

CORNISH STADIUM
ST. AUSTELL
Tuesday, 29th Aug, 1961
AT 7.45 P.M.

" CAPSTAN "
CIGARETTE TROPHY

Official Souvenir Programme 9d.

★★★★★★★★★★★★★★★★★★★★★★★★

A 1961 programme cover.

Clearly Trevor Redmond felt that speedway had no future in Neath and encouraged by the support he had received at the Cornish Stadium announced that St Austell would replace the Dragons in the 1963 Provincial League. It was a gamble for although it was generally considered that speedway in Cornwall was viable in the high summer season, doubts were expressed that the Gulls would attract sufficient support early in the season before the holidaymakers arrived. With this in mind Redmond delayed his opening home fixtures until May.

Plymouth had closed at the end of 1962, which gave Redmond the opportunity to snap up Cornish riders Chris Julian, Chris Blewett, and Ray Wickett and hopefully pull in some of the Devils' support. Redmond would continue to ride and had also intended to use Francis Cann who had been on loan at Exeter for two seasons but prior to the season Cann announced his retirement. He would eventually change his mind and continue to ride for the Falcons. From Neath came George Major and Glyn Chandler while another addition was Eastbourne junior Bob Warner. Finally Australian international Ray Cresp was signed as No.1.

The Gulls first track appearance was at Exeter on Monday 1 April where they lost 45-32 despite Redmond scoring a 12-point maximum. Two weeks later St Austell notched their first Provincial League victory at Long Eaton. Cresp was late returning from Australia, added to which the SCB were unhappy with a rider whom they considered a First Division heat leader racing in the lower division. The situation was clarified in time for Cresp to make his debut at Cradley where the Gulls drew 39-39 even though their new No.1 only managed to score 3 points. It was soon apparent that he was unhappy with the rough state of the Provincial League tracks, so much so that he fitted hydraulic forks to his machine.

A few days before the home season opened at Cornish Stadium, Blewett crashed spectacularly in the last race at Exeter and broke his arm. That first home match resulted in a 42-36 victory over Poole Pirates, the reigning League champions, in the Western Cup. Although Exeter won in this competition at Par Moor the following week, the Gulls quickly got into their stride, scoring home and away victories over New Cross Rangers before beating Exeter in the League. The home victory over the Rangers on Whit Monday saw Ray Cresp, Chris Julian and Glyn Chandler all score maximums, the latter registering his first ever full 12-point score.

George Major.

Sheffield Tigers would be the only team to take points away from the Cornish Stadium, winning 41-37 in June. The Gulls offset this loss by winning 44-34 at Rayleigh a few days later, where Chandler scored another maximum, and also took an away draw at Middlesbrough. Another ex-Plymouth Devil, Lew Philp, had been added to the Gulls' strength but sadly his career ended when he was seriously injured in an accident at Sheffield. Philp in turn was replaced by Rye House junior Mike Keen.

A wet summer caused fixture congestion late in the season, forcing Redmond to run twice a week in August by which time St Austell were challenging for the championship. The Gulls' hopes depended on them winning at Hackney, but a match they were expected to win resulted in a defeat thanks to a heavily over watered track. Edinburgh's George Hunter had already won the St Austell World Championship qualifying round, now Exeter's Jimmy Squibb won the Provincial League Riders qualifier, while Ivan Mauger top scored for the Overseas team which beat Britain 57-51 in the international series. The last League match at Par Moor saw the Gulls beat Long Eaton 49-29 with Julian scoring a 12-point maximum. The season ended on Tuesday 1 October when Cornwall beat Devon 33-21.

All together eighteen of the Gulls' home matches had been affected by rain but it had still generally been a successful season. Therefore it came as something of a shock to local supporters when Trevor Redmond announced that he would be moving his entire operation to Glasgow in 1964. Redmond had gone into partnership with Edinburgh promoter Ian Hoskins and would be the front man as Hoskins obviously did not want to be seen running the Monarchs' arch rivals. TR later joked that he had to make the move as he could not refuse the offer of an office with a telephone.

It would be another 34 years before League speedway was seen again in Cornwall. Stock car racing continued at Par Stadium under Redmond until the late eighties when the stadium was eventually demolished to make way for a supermarket. During the summer of 1996 rumours spread that a new track was being planned. The idea was the brainchild of Brian Annear, proprietor of St Blaizey Motorcycles. Annear had been follower of the Gulls at the Cornish stadium and his interest had continued, more recently, through sponsorship of Mark Simmonds at Exeter.

Annear had persuaded the massive English China Clay Company to allow him to build a speedway track at Longstone Pit at Nanpean. The site was used as an off-road facility for young offenders but was far from flat enough to be used for speedway. Nevertheless ECC were talked into dynamiting thousands of tons of rock and moving vast amounts of china clay before a 300m track could be laid in this unique moonscape high in the Cornish clay country.

Annear also persuaded his three sons, Andy, Steve and Jason, to help him with the project. All rode moto-cross but were not particularly interested in speedway. The plan was to relaunch the Gulls in the Conference League using local riders. On paper, the side that was assembled looked extremely weak, as the more experienced Cornish riders already rode for Exeter Falcons. Wayne Barrett had raced for Weymouth and Poole ten years earlier, while Callington's Mike Bowden was at the veteran stage, having ridden for several Conference League teams including Exeter. Mark Phillips and Darren Matthews also had limited speedway experience while grass trackers Jason Prynne,

Phillips' younger brother Simon and Chris Bennett were all keen to give it a go. Prynne's father Nigel would take on the duties of track manager and was soon regularly producing one of the best prepared race strips in the country.

The new Gulls were launched at a press and practice session but the event was over-shadowed by the death in a gyrocopter crash the previous day of the legendary Chris Julian. Chris had been delighted that speedway was about to return to Cornwall and would surely have been involved on race nights. St Austell's first match was against the high-flying Western Warriors at Exeter's County Ground stadium on spring bank holiday Monday. The Warriors expected an easy victory especially with the Lobb cousins, Roger and Gary, in their line-up, but the Gulls gave it a real go and were unlucky not to snatch a surprise win.

The opening meeting at the Clay Country Moto Parc was scheduled for Tuesday 2 June with a return match against the Warriors. A huge crowd, estimated at 3,000, flocked over the hill and into the stadium. All were overwhelmed by the amazing beauty of the rocky location and the deep aquamarine lake which lay at one end of the track. The popular view was that it resembled a location for the *Doctor Who* television series.

Such was the size of the crowd that presenter Dave Stallworthy had to extend the introductions to allow all the fans time to get in. The parade also highlighted the somewhat anarchic approach that the Annear family would take towards the speedway. While Exeter boss Colin Hill led his team out dressed in immaculate regulation red blazer, grey flannels and black shoes, Brian Annear roared out on a 50cc monkey bike wearing T-shirt, shorts and work boots!

It was immediately apparent that the new track would provide superb racing. The first race was won by Wayne Barrett, but the Warriors eventually won 41-34. The Gulls' third defeat came against Belle Vue Colts later that week after being kept waiting outside the stadium by Aces promoter John Perrin until after the Elite League match had finished. St Austell lost 48-29 on the ultra-slick track but Barrett scored an 18-point maximum which brought his tally in the first three matches to 45 points. Unfortunately Jason Prynne crashed and broke his collarbone, but made up for this later in the A&E department of the local hospital when he and Barrett suggested to the Annears that they ask former Exeter rider Steve Bishop to consider making a comeback. Bishop had dropped out of speedway and was now concentrating on continental long-track racing.

Bishop, a landscape gardener from Bristol, quickly agreed and made his debut against the Shuttle Cubs, a combined Long Eaton and Wolverhampton team. It was a memorable night as not only did 'Bish' score a 15-point maximum but the Gulls recorded their first victory, 53-25. Bishop also scored 14 at Buxton where the Gulls lost 40-32, then defeated Belle Vue 47-31 back at Nanpean. St Austell's first away win, a superb 50-28 victory over the Shuttle Cubs at notoriously difficult Wolverhampton track was achieved later that week. The combined Reading/Swindon team, the Raven Sprockets were the Gulls next victims at the Moto Parc with Bishop taking another 15-point maximum.

Bishop was away riding long-track the following weekend when the Gulls set out on the 500-mile journey to Berwick where they were beaten 54-24 by the League leaders. It was a different story the next day at Lathallan in Scotland where St Austell won 43-35

The Clay Country Moto Parc is covered by snow.

with Barrett netting 14. Travel fatigue obviously affected the Gulls riders' as the Buxton Hit Men scored a 41-37 victory at the Moto Parc the following Tuesday.

Another local rider Dean Garton replaced Bowden in the Gulls' line-up for the 55-21 win over the Anglian Angels, a combined Ipswich/King's Lynn team. By now the Peterborough Thundercats were being considered likely League champions and the Gulls discovered why when they were beaten 44-34 at the East of England show-ground. Back at the Moto Parc, St Austell hit the 50-point mark against both Berwick and Lathallan and then went to Oxford where they won by a single point, 39-38. The return match had to be abandoned when rain hit the Motoparc, but the score was allowed to stand at 43-11. Mike Bowden had joined the Ryde Wizards by the time the Isle of Wight-based team visited Cornwall. The Gulls won 45-33 but lost the return 43-35.

About this time Skegness co-promoters Peter Oakes and his daughter Sarah Gudgeon approached Brian Annear with a view to switching their Premier League Braves team to Cornwall. Annear gave their offer due consideration but decided to stick with the Conference League, while Skegness moved to the Isle of Wight instead. Peter Oakes soon returned to the Clay Country Moto Parc this time with his sensational Peterborough Thundercats for what promised to be the match of the season. The Cats had only suffered one defeat, at Exeter, and included such exciting prospects as 15-year-olds David Howe and Simon Stead, Ross Brady, Jason Bunyan and Oliver Allen. Not

£1.00

ST. AUSTELL SPEEDWAY

MEETING
NUMBER
97

BRITISH SPEEDWAY
AMATEUR LEAGUE
ST. AUSTELL GULLS
v
EXETER/NEWPORT
WESTERN WARRIORS
*Tuesday 3rd June 1997
at 7.30 p.m.*

A 1997 programme cover.

surprisingly a near 3,000 crowd turned up to watch the Gulls battle for every point in a meeting which the League leaders won by a single point, 39-38.

The Gulls completed a hectic week with a 40-38 away win over the Raven Sprockets at Swindon. Bishop won his first four races on the track at which he had begun his career but the chance of a maximum vanished when he forgot to turn his fuel on before his last outing. They then lost their penultimate away match at Mildenhall 48-30, but wrapped up their official home fixtures with a 40-38 win over the Fen Tigers. Their first League season back in harness concluded with a 44-34 victory over the Anglian Angels, which enabled them to finish their first year in a highly creditable sixth place.

That season the Conference tracks were limited to just twelve meetings. Although Annear applied to the BSPA to be allowed to stage a couple of charity meetings, one of which he planned to organise around the BBC's Children in Need, permission was refused. The season ended with a charity challenge match against an unofficial Exeter select, but not before Mark Simmonds, riding for the Isle of Wight, won the Cornish Grand Prix.

In 1997 several senior tracks had run a combined conference League team. For the following season this was not permitted in a bid to encourage successful independent tracks like St Austell to join the Premier League. Having previously turned down the approach by Skegness, Annear now found himself talking to Long Eaton promoters Graham Drury and Tony Mole when the Invaders found themselves without a home just three weeks before the start of the new season. Again the approach was refused as it was felt that such a move would jeopardise the future of the remaining tracks. It was a decision Annear would later regret.

For 1998 St Austell would be represented by a twelve-man squad. Leading the challenge for honours were Bishop and Barrett, supported by Prynne and the Phillips brothers, Mark and Simon. Mark had become known as the Undertaker after it was revealed that he was sponsored by a firm of funeral directors. This developed to such an extent that he even travelled to meetings in an old hearse. Chris Bennett, Ryan Deering, Jim Collins and Chris Dix were also included while ten-times Cornish moto-cross champion Seemond Stephens, who had tried speedway for the first time at the end of '97, and 15-year-old Chris Harris quickly began to make their mark. Former Warriors skipper Kevin Phillips moved west and the Gulls found another thrill maker in Australian Adrian Newman. Newman had arrived at Exeter but with no chance of a team place was advised to try his luck at St Austell.

The campaign began at Newport where the Gulls lost 53-33 to the newly named Mavericks, the side that would prove to be St Austell's main rivals for the next two years. Jim Collins failed to score on his debut for the Gulls and did not appear again. The home season opened with a Youth Development fixture against Exeter, followed by a challenge match against a makeshift Warriors line-up. The Gulls, by now sponsored by BWOC, the independent petrol company, won both matches. This meeting also proved to be Chris Bennett's last appearance in Gulls colours.

The Gulls rode in the final match at Skegness, before the Braves moved their operation for financial reasons to King's Lynn where they became known as the Norfolk Braves. To mark the occasion Wayne Barrett scored paid 17 in a resounding 51-38

Bronze helmet holder Steve Bishop is interviewed by Dave Stallworthy.

victory for the Gulls. A second victory over the Braves was achieved back at the Moto Parc where this time Barrett romped to a 15-point maximum.

Thanks to the huge support the Gulls had attracted in 1997 the BSPA had invited the Annear family to stage the Conference League Riders Final at St Austell. Every effort was put into making this a classic occasion, but by now it was already becoming evident that the crowds were not what they had been the previous year. Around 1,500 turned out for the CLRC which, due to a number of late withdrawals, almost became the Cornish championship. Not surprisingly the title was won by Steve Bishop whose main challenge came from Newport's Andrew Appleton, but the biggest surprise was the sparkling form of Gulls' Seemond Stephens who in only his first season finished third.

A much anticipated Knockout Cup clash with Newport resulted in a 59-31 win at the Moto Parc with Bishop scoring 17 and Stephens paid 12. Exeter's Roger Lobb, who's father Peter had played a major role in building the track, joined the Gulls for the away leg at Queensway Meadows. Lobb scored 13 but despite losing 52-38 the Gulls went through on aggregate 97-83.

Steve Bishop scored another 15-point maximum in the Gulls' 52-38 home victory over Mildenhall, while Lobb romped to an 18-point full house at Buxton where the Gulls won 53-35. Norfolk were then demolished 71-19 with Bishop, Lobb and Barrett all unbeaten by an opponent. The return at King's Lynn produced a 51-39 victory for the Gulls with Lobb paid for 18, this put the Gulls in the driving seat in the race for the League championship. The next day saw St Austell draw 45-45 at Mildenhall. Big home wins over the Fen Tigers and Newport clinched the Conference League title for the BWOC Gulls.

With the League and individual championship already in their possession the Gulls now turned to the Knockout Cup. They beat Mildenhall 53-38 in the first leg at the Clay Country Moto Parc and then went to West Row where St Austell gained their third trophy. The Gulls won 52-38 on the day and 105-76 on aggregate, with another new signing James Birkenshaw netting 13.

With speculation increasing that Annear was about to take St Austell into the Premier League, the Gulls discovered how tough life would be at that level when they entertained a full-strength Exeter Falcons line-up on Tuesday 6 October. The locals fought hard but in an all-action meeting which attracted a bumper crowd, Exeter stormed to a 59-30 victory.

The penultimate away match saw the Gulls win 53-36 at Buxton, while at the Moto Parc Falcons' Mark Simmonds retained his Cornish Grand Prix title. The season concluded with another away win this time at Newport where the Gulls won 54-35, but the afternoon ended acrimoniously when due to lack of serviceable machinery the St Austell riders declined to take part in a second-half event.

The early part of the winter saw Brian Annear engage in secret talks with Exeter promoter Colin Hill with the aim of forming a partnership which would give the Gulls Premier League status. But sadly after doing their sums they decided that the idea was financially unviable and abandoned it. Regrettably what had been the Gulls' most successful season results wise had also produced their poorest attendance figures.

The third season of speedway at the Clay Country Moto Parc saw the BWOC Gulls lose the services of Steve Bishop and exciting prospect Chris Harris. Bishop accepted a lucrative offer to ride for Premier League Swindon while Harris would fulfil his ambition by joining Exeter Falcons. Seemond Stephens had signed to ride for Eastbourne Eagles in the Elite League and doubts were expressed that he would still be eligible to race at Conference level. However by the time St Austell opened in May 1999 he too had switched to Premier League racing with Swindon so was allowed to double up.

Roger Lobb, now on loan to Arena Essex, was ruled out as his Premier League average was too high, but his cousin Gary agreed to race for the Gulls who opened the season with a 48-42 win at Mildenhall. This match also saw Richard Ford and Martin Williams make their Gulls' debut along with regular teamsters Wayne Barrett, Jason Prynne and Kevin Phillips. Adrian 'Skippy' Newman, fresh from a successful winter spent ice racing in the USA, overlooked the fact that his racing licence needed to be renewed and was prevented from competing by the referee.

League newcomers Rye House Rockets were track sharing with Mildenhall and planned to race the Gulls in the second half of a double-header but the second match never started due to the sudden arrival of heavy rain. The Fen Tigers gained swift revenge when they spoilt the Gulls' opening night by winning 47-43 at the Moto Parc. The high spot for St Austell was an 18-point maximum by Seemond Stephens, a score which was to launch a long run of unbeaten scores by the Newquay-based rider.

The Gulls maintained their excellent away form with a draw at Buxton despite their riders suffering a number of falls and injuries. Big home wins were recorded against Rye House and Linlithgow, while the restaged match against the Rockets at Mildenhall saw the Gulls notch their highest-ever away score, 62-28. King's Lynn were despatched 61-29 at the Moto Parc, and then Mildenhall were beaten 52-38 in the semi-final of the Knockout Cup. Hopes of retaining the championship took a severe blow at the start of August when the old enemy Newport won 47-43 in a match which also saw Stephens beaten by Mavericks' Bobby Eldridge, a rare occurrence that summer.

Chris Harris returned to the Moto Parc and won the Eclipse Grand Prix a week later before the darkness descended on Cornwall the following morning. The Gulls returned to winning ways when they beat Buxton 49-41, but their chance of victory at Linlithgow disappeared when the van carrying the management and several riders broke down on the M6 near Preston and was only repaired in time to reach the picturesque Heathersfield track as Stephens lost the Bronze Helmet at the conclusion of the match. The Gulls had been forced to draft in local juniors Gary Flint and Neil Stevens as replacements but still lost by only 2 points. Stephens was on form again the following day when he notched a 15-point maximum as the Gulls drew 45-45 at Mildenhall.

The next match was at Newport where the Gulls went down narrowly 48-42 as Martin Williams failed to score in three races on his former track. Mark Simmonds' hopes of completing a hat-trick of Cornish GP wins was thwarted by his Exeter team-mate Michael Coles. Despite winning their final away match at King's Lynn, St Austell had lost their League title to Newport, but after a gap of several weeks the Gulls refused to give up the Knockout Cup as well. They met the Mavericks in the final on a sunny October Sunday afternoon. Trailing by 14 points from the first leg St Austell fought their way

Action on the first bend.

back into contention, with Skippy Newman scoring a match winning 18, the Gulls cancelled out the deficit to win in style.

English China Clay, the Gulls landlords had, by now, been taken over by a giant French company Imreys, who informed the Annear family that they intended to restart working Longpit. There was no definite start date, but the Annear's lease would not be renewed at the end of 2000. A new location would have to be found and five alternative sites, including one on the approach road to what would become the Eden Project, were offered, but none materialised.

For 2000 the Conference League had gained three new teams, Peterborough, Sheffield and the Somerset Rebels, while Linlithgow had changed names yet again and become Glasgow Ashfield. Somerset promptly displaced Newport as the Gulls' arch-rivals when they tried to tempt Richard Ford away from the Moto Parc. Worse was to follow. All Cornwall had rejoiced when it became known that Steve Bishop was expected to return and lead the 2000 BWOC Gulls. But the celebrations were short-lived as later 'Bish' decided instead to sign for Somerset as it much nearer to his Bristol home. The Annears appreciated his reasoning and wished him luck but clearly serious rivalry would surround encounters between the Gulls and their new West Country neighbours.

The season opened with an away League Cup win at Buxton. Barrett scored 16 points and both Prynne and Williams reached double figures. But what would be a plague of injuries began when Gary Lobb crashed and hurt his arm. The injury would keep him out for over a month. The Gulls, using rider replacement for Lobb, comfortably won the return match at the Moto Parc to go through on aggregate. Barrett led the way with an 18-point maximum, Jason Prynne was paid for 16, and Martin Williams notched 11.

The next match against Boston was much closer due in the main to the fact that St Austell could only effectively track four riders. With rider replacement already in operation the Gulls were further depleted when Richard Ford crashed during the parade but St Austell scraped home 46-44. A week later Ashfield were beaten 52-36 with Williams netting 17, but Phelps crashed in his opening race as a result of which he was out for several weeks. Mark Thomson from Mildenhall made six appearances in the team but the highest score he managed was 4 points and Oxford's Darren Andrews was also signed, but he only appeared infrequently and failed to make an impression.

The long-awaited return of Steve Bishop along with the newly formed Somerset team came in the next round of the League Cup, which the Gulls won 48-40. The return at Highbridge a few days later was the Rebels opening match and saw St Austell suffer a hugely disappointing 55-35 defeat. Championship-chasing Mildenhall then won at the Moto Parc in a match which saw the re-emergence of Will James. James had quit a speedway career with Poole in the late eighties to concentrate on running his own hotel at Newquay, but now made a surprise come back.

The Gulls returned to winning ways with a string of victories at the Moto Parc. Buxton were beaten 51-38 but it was not enough to clinch the bonus point. Will James was quickly getting back into his stride and in only his third meeting scored 13 points. Rye House were dismissed 53-37 but again the winning margin was not sufficient to

Seemond Stephens leads ahead of Cradley guest, Chris Harris.

earn the bonus. Another injury victim Gary Phelps returned to action in time for the League visit of Somerset, but Martin Williams had now been injured riding for Stoke in the Premier League and would miss most of the season.

At Peterbrough's East of England showground St Austell were on course for victory in the final race until veteran Ian Barney and Jamie Smith carved their way through to snatch a last gasp 46-44 win. The return match at the Moto Parc was a very different story as the Gulls won 63-27 with only Barney offering any serious resistance.

The high spot of the season came at Somerset where the Gulls won 46-44 and this was followed up by a 57-33 victory over Boston in the Knockout Cup in which James scored a six-ride paid maximum. Newport were dismissed 55-33 but St Austell's hopes of retaining the Knockout Cup ended when Boston won the second leg at King's Lynn 65-25 for an aggregate 95-82 victory. The Gulls final home League match on 22 August saw them beaten 52-38 by Sheffield Prowlers who were now neck and neck with Mildenhall in the title race, a race in which the Gulls still had a part to play.

Meanwhile the St Austell season and indeed the Conference League era came to an end at the Clay Country Moto Parc on Tuesday 5 September with the Cornish Grand Prix. The rules now prohibited Premier League riders from taking part so the reigning champion Michael Coles was unable to defend his title. After fifteen races Gary Phelps topped the score chart with 12 points from his five rides, having been excluded for a tapes offence in his first race. He was joined in the final by Will James, Mildenhall's Shane Colvin and Jason Prynne.

At the first attempt James fell at the first corner, seriously damaging his own machine and Phelps' back wheel in the process. Colvin took full advantage to win the rerun from James with Prynne third while the unfortunate Phelps retired. Wayne Barrett represented the Gulls at the Conference League Riders Championship at Newport the following weekend where he finished fifth.

The Gulls lost 48-42 at Sheffield on 8 October but still had to visit Boston and Mildenhall in what had become an exceptionally wet autumn. St Austell travelled to King's Lynn for a mid-week staging of their match with Boston, only to find the stadium in darkness and the match postponed due to an important Elite League fixture the following evening. Plans to stage both matches at Mildenhall on the last weekend of the season were washed out by the weather on both Saturday and Sunday. The Fen Tigers desperately needed to beat the Gulls to clinch the Conference League title but the Cornish outfit were unable to track a team for the last available date in October but offered to return on the following Sunday. The BSPA refused to sanction the meeting as it was outside the official season and Sheffield duly took the title. An Elite League match was allowed to go ahead.

During the summer it became clear that a second speedway team was being planned for Cornwall. The Trelawny Tigers, run by a consortium of local enthusiasts, planned to stage Premier League racing at a track yet to be built. Clearly there was not enough support to sustain two speedway tracks in Cornwall. The Annear family tired from four hectic years relaunching the sport west of the Tamar and disillusioned by the end-of-season antics offered the Trelawny consortium the chance to take over at the Moto Parc. The offer was accepted and the JAG Tigers replaced the BWOC Gulls.

The new consortium, consisting of Godfrey Spargo, Peter Deering, Shirley Stephens, Ray Purvis and Mark Phillips, wasted no time in making sweeping changes to the Moto Parc. A new safety fence was installed and the famous old double-decker bus, which housed the referee's box, was replaced with portakabins. A canvas windbreak was erected on the back straight to make life more comfortable for the spectators on draughty evenings.

Team-building also began when Graeme Gordon was signed from Exeter to become not only the first Tiger but also the first Trelawny skipper. Gary Phelps agreed to continue and then another Falcon Chris Harris joined on loan to give the new team its first genuine Cornish rider. Two Germans, Steffan Mell and Marco Mueller, were the next riders to sign followed closely by Australian Brett Woodifield from Peterborough and a Czech youngster Pavel Ondrasik. To complete the team another Aussie Lee Herne was transferred from Newport.

The launch of Premier League racing was delayed first by the foot-and-mouth disease epidemic, as the Moto Parc was within MAFF's exclusion zone, nearly causing the Trelawny promoters to cancel the Tigers' Premier Trophy fixtures, and then by heavy rain which did cause the cancellation of the Tigers' opening match against Reading. At the restaging a week later all the work of the new consortium was proved worthwhile, Nigel Prynne's hand-laid and newly levelled race strip producing superb racing. Reading won that opening match 51-39 but everyone went home delighted by the quality of the racing. A week later the JAG Tigers achieved their first victory a narrow 46-44 win over Swindon. Several more home wins followed before high-flying Hull Vikings put Trelawny out of the Knockout Cup by inflicting home and away defeats.

The Tigers commenced their Premier League fixtures by beating Berwick Bandits 52-38 at the start of June by which time team changes had already been made. Ondrasik had picked up a knee injury which would trouble him all season in that first win against Swindon. Although he continued to ride Wayne Barrett was not so lucky. The former Gull had begun the season at reserve but broke his wrist at Sheffield and was replaced by another former St Austell rider, Simon Phillips. In early July the highly experienced Mark Courtney became available from Glasgow, when they signed Danish rider Henning Bager, who had previously been a Trelawny target. Phelps was dropped and replaced by a new Swedish signing Kenny Olsson, who quickly mastered the Moto Parc only to be sidelined by a serious knee injury at Arena Essex.

Chris Harris had been enjoying a highly successful season culminating with his qualification as reserve for the World Under-21 Final at Peterborough. Shortly afterwards he fractured his wrist at Stoke and was also out for the remainder of the year. Another hopeful from the Czech Republic, Richard Wolff, came over to replace him but by now the JAG Tigers were condemned to finish in the lower reaches of the Premier League table, one slot above wooden spoonists Newport.

The Trelawny promoters' original plan had been to build their own track on land at Hendra Farm, Mitchell, just off the A30, and towards the end of the 2001 season a planning application was entered. Despite considerable support from not only local speedway fans but many in other parts of the country, the application was unfortunately turned down. This seriously threatened the Tigers' future as their tenancy of the

Chris Harris.

Pavel Ondrasik.

Moto Parc was only for one year. Thanks to encouragement from the Mayor of St Austell, Councillor Joan Vincent, landowners Imreys granted the speedway a further extension.

Having survived their first season of Premier League and with the threat of home-lessness lifted, the Trelawny management set about building their team for 2002. Brett Woodifield was ruled out through work permit difficulties, and both Mark Courtney and Graeme Gordon were released. Agreement was reached with Colin Hill for Chris Harris to continue on loan, and with Exeter's future in doubt Seemond Stephens decided to return to his former home. Argentinian Emiliano Sanchez moved to Cornwall in an exchange deal which took Kenny Olsson to Glasgow, and Swindon asset Steve Masters was signed on loan after a disappointing season at Newport. Trelawny's two Czech riders Pavel Ondrasik and Richard Wolff both returned, along with local reserve Simon Phillips.

The JAG Tigers began the season with a notable away win at Exeter in the Premier Trophy. Newly appointed skipper Seemond Stephens led by example at his old track with 14 points while Richard Wolff, his original assessed 9-point average having dropped to 5 thus making him eligible to ride at No.6, chipped in with a useful 10 points. Having won all their home Premier Trophy matches and gained a draw at Somerset, Trelawny headed their group and went on to beat Reading home and away in the semi-finals. By then Stephens had injured tendons in his hand which kept him out of action for several weeks.

The home leg of the Premier Trophy final saw the Tigers hammer their namesakes from Sheffield 63-27. Trelawny would need that lead in Yorkshire as the Pirtek Tigers were unbeatable around their own big pacy Owlerton track and would go on to win the League championship and the Knockout Cup. Although Sheffield came storming back and gave the Cornish outfit a mauling in the second leg Trelawny just managed to hold on and win on aggregate by 3 points.

Trelawny looked set to continue their winning form in the Premier League when the JAG Tigers claimed an early away win at Glasgow. The highly experienced Alun Rossiter replaced Stephens for eight matches until he returned from injury at the beginning of July. Press speculation predicted that the Tigers' skipper was about to rejoin Exeter, and this proved correct although Stephens helped Trelawny to win at Stoke once again becoming a Falcon. Veteran Australian Tony Primmer who had last ridden for Milton Keynes in the early nineties was brought in as a replacement but only lasted five matches before being dropped. Another former Gull, Jason Prynne, returned after Pavel Ondrasik broke his shoulder while racing in the Czech championship, and Richard Wolff, after his fine run in the Premier Trophy, was out for several weeks with a broken hand. Another injury victim was Simon Phillips. These injuries meant that Trelawny were unable to maintain the momentum and gradually slipped down the table to eventually finish fourteenth out of seventeen. While the second half of the season proved less successful than the first there was nothing disappointing about the form of Chris 'Bomber' Harris. During the year he matured noticeably as a rider and again topped the Trelawny averages. The icing on the cake proved to be a superb fourth place in the World Under-21 Championship final in the Czech Republic.

Towards the end of the season pressure of business forced Peter Deering to resign leaving Godfrey Spargo as the sole promoter. The Trelawny Tigers were now an established Premier League team and the superbly maintained Clay Country Moto Parc track rated as one of the very best race strips in Britain. Sadly 2002 ended with Spargo seeking a new location for the JAG Tigers following the news that the unique little track will eventually be lost due to the demands of the china clay industry.

PART IV

POOLE AND RINGWOOD

POOLE

For more than fifty years Poole Speedway has been rightly regarded as one of Britain's most successful tracks. The Pirates have won numerous championships and been consistently well-supported but few of their fans realise that the very existence of the team is due in the main to several Dorset and Hampshire-based riders racing for Exeter in 1947. These early Falcons included Tom Crutcher, Sid 'Hap' Hazzard, Alan Chambers and the Hayden brothers, Herbie and Charlie. Travel was not easy in those post-war days and they decided that they wanted a track nearer home. Plans were initially formulated to stage speedway in Bournemouth's Kings Park until eventually an application to lease Poole Stadium was approved.

On Tuesday 6 January 1948, Poole Council accepted an offer of £1,000 per year for a ten-term lease, and Poole Speedway Ltd was officially formed the following month. The team would be nicknamed the Pirates, in recognition of the town's buccaneering heritage. Naturally the Pirates symbol would be the skull and crossbones on a blue background.

Tragically Poole's intended managing director Tom Crutcher was killed in a road accident shortly before Christmas 1947, when he fell a sleep at the wheel of his lorry while delivering a load of festive holly in Surrey. His brother Jack and Herbie Hayden continued the plans, while Clifford Brewer, a local builder, and Ron Bear took Tom's place becoming general manager and club secretary respectively.

The track at Wimborne Road originally bore similarities to Exeter in that it was originally a cycle track and to begin with was surrounded by a steel safety fence. The concrete cycle track was ripped up before the shale could be laid while a post-war shortage of materials meant that the original safety fence was constructed from steel sheets. Lack of money also meant that the fence had to be painted by 200 volunteer schoolboys, who completed the job in one day!

Charlie Hayden, Alan Chambers and Sid Hazzard were all named in the team for the opening National Trophy match away at Tamworth. Alf Elliott had been signed from Sheffield, Fred Pawson and Sid Clarke from Harringay, along with ex-Wimbledon rider, George Butler, while local grass tracker Bingley Cree completed the line-up. It was not an auspicious start for the Pirates who lost 63-21. Ten days later tragedy marred the opening night when Charlie Hayden and Yarmouth's Reg Craven collided on the first turn of the first race. Alf Elliott following close behind was unable to avoid the fallen riders and crashed into them. Elliott walked away, but both Hayden and Craven were taken to hospital, where Craven died eight days later, without regaining consciousness.

The Pirates went on to win 74-32 and from then on Poole Speedway never looked back. A run of injuries prevented them from making much of an impression that first season; George Gower was the first to go with a broken leg, Alf Elliott next having fractured ribs and a wrist. Joe Bowkis broke a collarbone and ribs in a match race with

Tom Crutcher, 'the Pirate that never was'.

Gil Blake, and then Cyril Quick, brought in on loan from Bristol to help fill the gaps, broke a leg in a grass-track meeting, having scored 11 points in his only appearance for the Pirates. Poole only managed tenth in the table that first season, but the support was good with average crowds of 7,000 while the local derby with Southampton attracted 9,600 supporters.

The Pirates finished sixth in 1949 and with a little more strength at reserve could have progressed even further. Quick returned from his broken leg and became a permanent Poole asset, having been purchased from Bristol for £200, while Dick Howard was signed from Hanley. Alan Chambers topped the Pirates' averages with Fred Pawson and Charlie Hayden providing solid support. Two other locally based riders, Frank Holcombe and 'Ticker' James began to make their mark along with a name that would become very familiar to Pirates' fans, Terry Small.

Injury forced Sid Hazzard to retire and in 1950 he became speedway manager at Wimborne Road. The year would be a good one for the Pirates and laid the foundation for Poole's long-term future. An Australian, Alan Wall, was signed, but much more significantly the Pirates' management purchased Ken Middleditch from Hasting for £800. The Londoner arrived in Poole with nowhere to live, but quickly found accommodation with one of his new locally based team-mates, Tony Lewis, who was just beginning his career. Middleditch and Lewis formed a partnership that became universally known as 'Me and My Shadow'. Alan Kidd, another long-serving Pirate, also made his Poole debut that summer. After losing to Liverpool 43-41 in their opening home League match, the Pirates kept a clean slate at Wimborne Road to finish second to Oxford in the Third Division table.

POOLE SPEEDWAY

THE STADIUM
POOLE

MONDAY, 23rd AUGUST, 1948

Official Programme 6ᵈ

A 1948 programme cover.

While the excitement of being title contenders unfolded on the track, promoter Cliff Brewer was playing his own games behind the scenes in 1951. Brewer had applied to Poole Council for a 73 per cent reduction in the rent he paid to lease the stadium. When the Council refused, Brewer threatened to close down the speedway, claiming that he had lost £400 in 1950. Poole Council clearly felt that the sport had a future and put the rights to stage speedway out to tender. Brewer made a late bid to carry on at the 1950 rate, but instead two councillors Geoffrey Bravery and Len Matcham took over. The new promotion put great emphasis on team spirit and public participation and their efforts were handsomely rewarded.

Middleditch became the captain and the Pirates also benefited from the inclusion of teenage sensation Brian Crutcher. Crutcher, the son of the late Tom, started out at the Ringwood training track, but burst on to the scene in Poole's fifth home match against Exeter. Just 16 and needing his mother to sign a release allowing him to ride, 'The Nipper', as he became known, won his first two races. As the Pirates held sufficient lead over their championship rivals, Crutcher was given a third outing against the Falcons' heat leader, Don Hardy. He won that race too, and from then on was never out of the Pirates' line-up. By the end of the season 'Nipper' was scoring maximums and had even ridden in a test match.

Rayleigh and Exeter had made the early running in the championship, but the Pirates, thanks to several stunning performances came through to lift the title despite a strong challenge from the Falcons.

Poole had also been strengthened early on by the arrival from Southampton of Roy Craighead and Bill Holden. Of their thirty-six League matches the Pirates lost only to Exeter (twice), Long Eaton, Plymouth and Cardiff. The Pirates were also victorious in the Festival of Britain Shield where they again edged out Exeter.

The Pirates were promoted to the Second Division in and simply carried on where they had left off in 1951. Jimmy Squibb replaced Charlie Haydon, but there were few other changes. So few in fact that the Pirates' No.9, the Scotsman Johnny Thomson, only had seven outings all season.

Ken Middleditch.

Tony Lewis and Ken Middleditch lead Sune Karlsson and Eric French at New Cross in 1953.

Poole began the season with a superb run in the *Daily Mail* National Trophy. They started the Second Division rounds with a 118-98 victory over Plymouth, winners of the Southern League rounds. Next the Pirates defeated Oxford and then Glasgow at White City in the Second Division Final. Against First Division opposition, Poole first beat Norwich 109-107 on aggregate before finally losing to New Cross 111-105.

In the League the Pirates swept all before them. They opened with a sensational 58-25 victory over Liverpool Chads at the Stanley Stadium, before moving on to Scotland where they beat the Edinburgh Monarchs. At home Poole were supreme, frequently achieving run-away wins; in eleven of the their twenty-two League matches at Wimborne Road they exceeded 60 points, topped the 50 mark nine times, with only Oxford and Edinburgh restricting the Pirates to 40 or more.

Crutcher, at just 17 years old, put the icing on the cake by becoming the first Poole rider to reach the Wembley World Final. More than 2,000 Pirates fans travelled up to the Empire Stadium to see him finish eleventh with 6 points.

Despite such outstanding all-round success, Poole were denied promotion to the First Division, due to the commonly held belief that south west tracks were geographically too distant from the hub of the sport in those pre-motorway days.

The Pirates remained in the Second Division for 1953, and narrowly missed out on a second successive championship. Away from home Poole became a huge attraction as the Pirates were guaranteed to provide a close and exciting match, but at home the certainty of big wins resulted in declining attendances. At Leicester and Wolverhampton, the Pirates lost by a single point, while at Motherwell and Stoke the final score line was 43-41 in favour of the home team. As a result of these close

Brian Crutcher battles for the lead at Oxford.

defeats, felt by many to have been caused by questionable refereeing decisions, Coventry won the championship from Poole by a single League point. Suspect refereeing decisions may have contributed towards Poole missing out on a possible hat-trick of championships but there was another more likely reason. The Pirates had also lost Brian Crutcher, who was transferred to First Division Wembley Lions early in the season. Crutcher, without doubt the greatest rider to come out of Poole, had asked the promoters for £500 to purchase a vehicle. The request was denied, and three days later he joined Wembley, where he received £1,250. Buster Brown joined the Pirates in exchange.

The Pirates were runners-up again in 1954, this time missing out to Bristol, with Bill Holden pushing Middleditch for the No.1 slot. Norman Strachan had become a regular team member and his scores compensated to some extent for a weakness at reserve, which led to a drop in away success.

1955 brought further championship success, but it was a season marred by tragedy. E.J.P. Rapson took over as team manager and a virtually unchanged Pirates side opened the campaign with a 74-33 victory over touring side Stockholm, at Easter. Poole showed that they meant business by going to Southampton and winning 61-35 and from then on the Pirates were virtually unstoppable. They suffered a major blow in May when Johnny Thomson crashed during a National Trophy match with Ipswich and suffered a broken thigh. Four days later he died in hospital as a result of an embolism.

Poole remained unbeaten at home and having notched up seven away victories, comfortably won the League championship by eight points from Coventry, thus gaining revenge over the Bees for their 1953 defeat. The Pirates also enjoyed another successful National Trophy run. Having beaten Rayleigh home and away in the first round, the Pirates overcame the Johnny Thomson tragedy by defeating Ipswich on aggregate. Swindon inflicted a 62-46 defeat at Blunsdon so the Pirates had to work hard to win the return leg 68-40 at Wimborne Road for another aggregate victory. After overcoming Southampton, Poole lost away to First Division Birmingham (56-52) but managed to force an aggregate draw at Wimborne Road. The replay took place in August. Again Birmingham won the first leg (67-41) but Poole fought back to win 69-39 and earn themselves a place in the semi-finals. By now the end of season fixture congestion was taking its toll, and Poole lost 82-26 at Norwich. This time there was no fight back and although the Pirates managed to beat the Stars by 8 points, it was not sufficient to reach the final.

Poole undertook a post-season tour of Denmark and Sweden, where again tragedy struck. Tony Lewis crashed during a match at Stockholm and fractured his skull. It seemed his career was over.

By 1956 the Pirates could no longer be denied and finally reached the First Division, the only team ever to climb to the top from Division Three on merit alone. For once the Pirates did not take the step in their stride. Although they were among the front runners in the early stages, Poole eventually dropped down to finish sixth out of seven, although well clear of the bottom club Bradford. Several of the regular Pirates soon found it tough going, but Middleditch soon adapted to the highest level.

Australian Jack Biggs was allocated to Poole. Initially unhappy about the move, preferring a London track, he eventually agreed to sign and thereafter enjoyed an excellent season in which he became the Pirates' top scorer. Cyril Roger was signed from Norwich, while his brother Bert joined from West Ham. Sadly Bert failed to recapture the form that had made him a big star at New Cross, but Cyril proved to be a quality heat leader. Norman Strachan missed most of the season after seriously injuring his hand

'The Nipper' – Brian Crutcher.

A 1956 programme cover.

while working in a saw mill while Bill Holden failed to adapt to the higher level of racing, and rejoined Southampton. As a result, former Exeter No.1 Jack Geran was persuaded to return to Britain from Australia, but arrived too late to make much difference to Poole's final lowly League position.

Matcham and Bravery withdrew the Pirates from the National League in early 1957, claiming that petrol rationing, introduced as a result of the Suez crisis, would cause a further decline in their already dwindling crowds. Jack Crutcher returned to take control, but unfortunately the Speedway Control Board insisted that track alterations be made first. As the work was estimated to cost in excess of £2,000 Crutcher declined to do so and instead staged open-licence racing. Meanwhile Rayleigh promoter Vic Gooden was struggling to keep his team in business and in the hope of attracting larger crowds staged two of the Rockets' League matches at Wimborne Road. Rayleigh, already bottom of the League, lost first to Belle Vue then Norwich. Gooden insisted that the arrangement would not be permanent, but in January 1958 he purchased Poole Speedway for £1,000, having agreed that 6 per cent of that season's gate receipts would go to the local council as rent for the stadium.

The Pirates' return to the National League brought little success and they finished ninth, one place above bottom team Ipswich. Jack Biggs was again allocated to Poole, and once more the Australian ended the season as top scorer. After a struggle, Gooden was given permission to use Birger Forsberg while Ken Middleditch was allowed to return from Swindon to boost the struggling Pirates. To add to the difficulties Forsberg and Les McGillivray were both injured, while Jack Unstead did not find the new track to his liking. To round off a dismal season Middleditch retired at the end of the summer.

1959 was another disappointing year at Poole. Biggs, never fully fit, failed to maintain his high-scoring form and new signing Ray Cresp took over as top man in a side which lacked a genuine No.1.

The fifties ended with another change of management when Southampton supremo Charles Knott took control at Poole in a move which would lead to the Pirates again becoming one of Britain's major speedway teams. In 1960 they joined the newly formed Provincial League. Major alterations and improvements were made to the stadium, including the construction of a new grandstand, which delayed the start of the season until June. Knott quickly assembled a useful side including Ross Gilbertson, and an impressive new Australian, Geoff Mudge. The Pirates were further strengthened when Knott brought back Ken Middleditch and then Tony Lewis. At first Poole were wary of Lewis making a comeback, but Cradley gave him second-half rides when Poole were the visitors. Tony won two races, and the Pirates snapped him up again.

Unfortunately a defeat at Stoke, before the return of Middleditch and Lewis, proved decisive for Poole who were battling with Rayleigh and Bristol for the championship, and Pirates had to settle for the runners-up spot.

With a settled team consisting of Middleditch, Lewis, Gilbertson, Mudge, Strachan and Kidd, the Pirates stormed to the 1961 championship. Poole were now so strong that Peter Vandenberg was moved to Southampton with Tim Bungay replacing him at

The 1961 Poole Pirates. From left to right, back row: Ron Hart (manager), Tony Lewis, Geoff Mudge, Tim Bungay. Front row: Ross Gilbertson, Ken Middleditch, Alan Kidd, Norman Strachan.

reserve. The Pirates won fifteen of their twenty matches and drew at Edinburgh. Their four defeats came at Middlesbrough, Plymouth, Rayleigh and Sheffield. At the end of the season Middleditch again announced his retirement.

Poole retained the championship in 1962. Mudge took over at No.1 and as captain, and Roy Trigg signed on loan from Wimbledon. Middleditch came out of retirement for one final match and scored 10 points against Bradford. The Pirates were again developing their own pool of junior talent and with an eye to the future preferred to give opportunities to Pete Smith, Pete Munday, Brian Leonard and Keith Whipp rather than sign more established riders.

1963 was a bridging year as the go-ahead Poole promotion eased in the new generation to take over from their long serving old guard. Gilbertson took over as highest scorer ahead of Mudge. Pete Smith, who had made his mark in the second half in '62, moved into the team proper, but Brian Leonard, for whom Poole held high hopes, broke his leg early on. Although the Pirates remained unbeaten at home in the Provincial League and also won away at Middlesbrough and Hackney, their failure to win at Sheffield and St Austell cost them the chance of a third championship, and they eventually finished third, their lowest placing in four seasons. Sheffield also spoilt Poole's home record by winning 52-44 in the Knockout Cup.

Poole's new generation developed slowly in 1964. The Pirates started well by winning eight of their twelve Southern League matches, but failed to maintain their winning form. Neither Pete Smith or Pete Munday made the progress expected of them, while Geoff Mudge and Ross Gilbertson struggled to maintain their usual form. Illness restricted Tony Lewis's scoring ability while Tim Bungay first retired, then changed his mind and joined Exeter. Hackney and Newport both won at Wimborne Road, while Poole failed to record a single away victory. Consequently the Dorset team dropped half-way down the table to sixth.

Poole returned to the highest level in 1965 when the breakaway Provincials merged with the old Nationals to form the new British League. The Pirates went into the new era without Tony Lewis, who had retired. Mudge and Gilbertson were joined by two New Zealanders, steeplechase jockey Bill Andrew and his protégé, Bruce Cribb. Ronnie Genz was signed from Oxford while Pete Smith, Brian Leonard and Pete Munday contested the reserve berths until Leonard left to join West Ham after just a couple of matches.

Poole's British League career began with four away matches, from which the Pirates gained wins at Wolverhampton and Oxford plus a draw at Swindon. After that sensational start they only managed to add one further away victory, at Long Eaton in May, although they came close at several other tracks. Injuries played a large part in this, Mudge being sidelined for a month after crashing on Easter Monday, while Strachan was hurt at Wimborne Road in July and missed the rest of the season.

Genz and Andrew scored well for the Pirates and both qualified for the British Final of the World Championship, while Pete Smith at last fulfilled his true potential. The Pirates finished tenth in the inaugural British League but only managed to beat Edinburgh in the Knockout Cup before going out to Wolverhampton.

The consolidation continued in 1966, and although stalwart Ross Gilbertson quit to develop his business, Ken Middleditch returned as team manager. Andrew, Genz and Mudge continued to head the team supported by Smith and Bruce Cribb. Two more New Zealanders, Colin McKee, and Wayne Briggs also moved to Dorset.

While the Pirates made steady progress in the League, climbing to sixth place, thanks to away wins at Cradley, King's Lynn and Belle Vue, and draws at Newport and Oxford, they also lost home matches to Swindon and Newcastle. The Knockout Cup jinx struck again. After beating Newcastle in the second round, the Pirates went on to win against Coventry, but the match was rerun following a protest and the Bees won the replay 49-46.

Bill Andrew took a year out in 1967 and stayed 'down under' to race horses. To replace him the Pirates signed Swede Gote Nordin, from Newport along with his Wasps team-mate Geoff Penniket. Colin Mckee was re-allocated to Hackney and Wayne Briggs, who after considering retirement moved to

Geoff Mudge.

Pete Smith.

Bill Andrew and Ronnie Genz.

Exeter. Mudge, Genz, Strachan, Smith and Cribb completed the line-up which was maintained throughout thanks to an injury-free season. When Nordin returned to home to fulfil Swedish commitments, his place was taken by Tony Lewis.

Nordin quickly became a huge favourite with Pirates fans, averaging 10 points a match and equalling the track record, a week after Ivan Mauger had broken it. The team continued to enjoy good home results. Poole lost only to Belle Vue while Edinburgh forced a draw, but away successes proved harder to come by. Their travels only netted a brace of draws, at Oxford and Glasgow, and a sole narrow 39-38 victory at Cradley. Nevertheless the Pirates finished a creditable sixth in the League but life would not be so comfortable in 1968.

Bill Andrew's return to Britain put the Pirates among the serious contenders for British League honours. Andrew was expected to form a powerful spearhead with Gote Nordin, but Poole's hopes were shattered when after just one match Nordin announced that he was returning to Sweden to concentrate on his business interests. Ronnie Genz, Norman Strachan and Geoff Penniket had all joined other tracks during the winter, and the Pirates stood little chance of finding another 10-point man at that early stage of the season. Instead, as the result of a tip-off, they brought in an unknown Norwegian, Odd Fossengen, as a stop gap in the hope of signing Czechoslovakian Antonin Kasper.

Fossengen made an instant impact on the fans, to such an extent that when the Poole management attempted to drop him in favour of Kasper, they launched a petition to keep him at Wimborne Road. In return Fossengen, in what should have been his last race, came good, scoring 10 points at West Ham. From then on the Pirates faced a battle to avoid the wooden spoon. Thanks to a tremendous team spirit, the Poole riders fought their way out of the doldrums, but suffered a further setback when Andrew broke his ankle in the British Final and ended his season prematurely. Pete Smith meanwhile found his form and in spite of the injury crisis that renowned team spirit lifted the Pirates two slots off the bottom of the table to finish in seventeenth place.

After such a difficult season the Pirates' fortunes were bound to change and they enjoyed a virtually injury free campaign in 1969. With just the addition of Australian Gordon Guasco and ably managed by Ron Hart the Pirates won all their home matches and also scored eight away victories and a draw. It was enough to see them once again end a season as champions, six points clear of second place Belle Vue.

The season began with a narrow aggregate win over Exeter in the Easter Trophy before the British League campaign opened with a home win over Newport and home and away successes against Swindon. The draw came at Glasgow in May, and Pirates also returned victorious from West Ham, Oxford, Exeter, Hull, Newcastle, Wolves and Newport. Sadly a defeat at Sheffield in July in the Knockout Cup ended Poole's hopes of achieving the double. It was a memorable year as Poole made history by becoming the first team ever to win League championships in three divisions, and Pete Smith ended the '60s by topping the Pirates averages for the first time. Geoff Mudge won the Poole World Championship qualifying round, while England beat Australia 66-42 in a test match at Wimborne Road and the Pirates won a challenge match against Norway.

Sadly Poole were unable to maintain the balance of their side in 1970, even though only one rider, Bruce Cribb, was forced to leave Wimborne Road to comply with rider control. Cribb moved west to Exeter and in exchange Mike Cake joined Poole.

The new decade opened with a win over Exeter in the Easter Trophy but a week later the reigning champions lost at home to the newly reformed Wembley Lions by 4 points. Wins over Cradley and King's Lynn were the Pirates' only successes in their first seven League matches. Smith, Mudge and Guasco all struggled, with the result that when the usually reliable Fossengen had a rare off-night there was nobody to cover for him. By mid-season the team's fortunes began to improve and Poole won seven of their next eight matches. Although Ted Leasing was sidelined for much of the season, with a broken ankle, the other Pirates all managed to avoid serious injury. Away from Dorset, Poole won at Hackney, Newport, Swindon and Sheffield, finally finishing fifth in the British League.

During the winter Gordon Guasco was killed while racing in Australia. This tragic event was followed by the news that long-serving Pirate Geoff Mudge had put in an unexpected transfer request, and that Ted Laessing had been moved to Oxford by the rider control committee. On top of all this Poole's promising No.7 Frank Shuter informed the management that he would be staying at home in New Zealand.

A 1971 programme cover.

John Langfield.

This left just three riders, so for 1971 the Poole bosses set about rebuilding their team. Norway's Reidar Eide, Swede Bo Wirebrand and colourful Aussie John Langfield were all drafted in to join Pete Smith, Odd Fossengen and Mike Cake. Langfield was reputed to have got lost en route to Poole but managed to arrive in time for the traditional Good Friday match against Exeter. Despite Langfield's fence scrapping tactics the Falcons' won 41-35. Reidar Eide proved a good captain and although he took a little time to settle in went on to top the Poole averages. Wirebrand also proved his worth even though he had also to cope with frequently commuting to and from his Swedish fixtures during the first half of the season. The Pirates lost three times at home and drew against Reading. On the road they won three times, at Glasgow, Leicester and Wembley and drew at King's Lynn. These successes did not prevent Poole from dropping into the bottom half of the table where they eventually finished eleventh. The Pirates also lost to Oxford in the first round of the *Speedway Star* Knockout Cup.

The Poole fans had a new hero to cheer in 1972 when exciting Swede Christer Lofqvist arrived at Poole from defunct West Ham to replace Reidar Eide. Lofqvist joined a line-up which already included Odd Fossengen, Pete Smith, John Langfield, Brian Collins, Mike Cake and Frank Shuter, and was believed strong enough to give the Pirates an outside chance of the title. This proved correct and although they only made it to seventh place, it was still an improvement on the previous year.

Three home matches were lost, to Belle Vue, King's Lynn and Reading, while Sheffield forced a draw. Away from home they won at Oxford and Newport and drew at Coventry. In September Lofqvist became the first Poole rider to compete in a Wembley world final since Brian Crutcher in 1952. Christer finished fourth and had previously also enjoyed a brief spell as holder of the Golden Helmet. He beat Jim MacMillan at Glasgow in June, but lost out to Ole Olsen a week later. Ever mindful for the future, Poole gave several young riders, including Martin Yeates, their first opportunity to race in the British League.

1973 saw more new additions arrive at Wimborne Road. Antonin Woryna was brought over from Poland and Jim Ryman, a top Second Division rider, was signed from Boston after making a few appearances for the Pirates the previous summer, while popular Swede Bo Wirebrand rejoined after a year's break. Once again it looked like a promising line-up, but any hopes of success were immediately hit by a run of injuries which saw Mike Cake damage his knee, Woryna break his wrist, Collins his nose, and Smith injure an ankle.

Despite these difficulties Poole began the British League campaign with an away draw at Swindon, a home win and then a victory at Hackney. The next home match saw Oxford draw and a week later Reading won at Wimborne Road. As the injuries crisis continued six more teams would inflict defeat on the Pirates on home shale. Long-serving Norman Strachan was recalled to help plug the gaps, while two young-sters Martin Yeates and top West Country karter Dave Buttigieg made several team appearances. No less than ten other riders made appearances in the Pirates' line-up including veteran Jimmy Squibb. To add to Poole's problems Wirebrand and Lofqvist were frequently required to miss matches due to their Swedish racing commitments. Subsequently those early season expectations were again dashed as the Pirates dropped to finish fourteenth in the British League table.

By 1974 the Pirates had gone from being a local team to a truly cosmopolitan outfit and Pete Smith was now the sole survivor of the '69 championship side. A ban on commuting Swedes meant there was no place for Lofqvist and Wirebrand. New

additions were Eric Broadbelt, signed from Belle Vue, Norwegian Oyvind Berg, Malcolm Ballard, and Richard May who came on loan from Reading. Polish red tape had to be overcome before Woryna could return to Wimborne Road.

No sooner had the season begun than Poole again hit difficulties. Ballard demanded a move after just three matches and the Pirates quickly replaced him with veteran Colin Gooddy. Berg failed to arrive for the start of the season and when he did eventually appear almost immediately returned home. Fortunately Woryna had received clearance to ride but tragedy struck at Oxford when the Rebels' Ulf Lovaas ran into the back of compatriot Odd Fossengen, breaking the Pirate's thigh. Less than a month later Eric Broadbelt fractured his ankle and was

Christer Lofqvist.

Neil Middleditch.

sidelined for two months. Until that point he and Pete Smith had held the team together with Gooddy's form proving an unexpected bonus. To add to Poole's woes Mike Cake also broke his ankle.

Yeates was used on a number of occasions and another youngster, Neil Middleditch, son of Ken, made his Poole debut. Not surprisingly Poole again finished fourteenth. The year ended with the death of Charlie Knott senior, at the age of 84, who had been responsible for the rebuilding of the stadium and the revitalisation of Poole Speedway in 1960.

Sadly the Pirates' fortunes did not improve in 1975 despite the arrival of what many feel was the most popular Poole rider of them all, Malcolm Simmons. Simmons was allocated to Poole from King's Lynn to give the Pirates a star-quality No.1. They also gained the highly spectacular Swede Christer Sjosten and an Aussie, Neil Cameron, who was expected to do well on big tracks. Neil Middleditch was given more opportunities, and rode in the majority of the Poole matches while continuing to double up with National League Eastbourne. Sadly Pete Smith's form dropped to such an extent that he retired and his replacement West German Christoph Betzl struggled at British League level. Cameron too proved a disappointment, failing to score in nine of his thirty-five appearances.

The year 1976 belonged to Malcolm Simmons. 'Super Simmo' had become the hero of the Poole fans and while the Pirates did not enjoy tremendous on track success, his efforts alone gave the supporters plenty to cheer about as he scored fourteen maximums for the Pirates. Once the international front Simmons became British champion before going on to finish second to his England team-mate Peter Collins in the World Final at Katowice, Poland. He also teamed up with John Louis to win the World Pairs championship.

Poole finished tenth in the League but injuries to both Eric Broadbelt and veteran Colin Gooddy early in the season hampered their bid for success. With Broadbelt out,

Martin Yeates was given plenty of rides as No.8. Neil Middleditch became a full-time Pirate and although he was ever present, he found the move to the higher division tough going. Pete Smith's career was now clearly coming to an end but he neverthe-less enjoyed a sell-out testimonial meeting. Richard May returned to Wimborne Road after a season back at Reading but failed to achieve consistency so Simmons' main support came from Christer Sjosten, whose thrilling and often reckless style frequently got him into trouble.

Simmons and Sjosten were joined in 1977 by Kevin Holden, nephew of fifties Pirate, Bill, and it was hoped that this would create a team capable of putting the Pirates back at the top. Holden had been transferred from Exeter and immediately looked set to fulfil his undoubted potential. He scored his first Poole maximum against Wimbledon in the Spring Gold Cup followed by paid double-figure scores in his next two matches. Then tragedy struck on 27 April, when in the second leg of the Knockout Cup match with Reading, 27-year-old Kevin crashed while attempting to overtake an opponent and was killed. The meeting was abandoned and the rest of the season was overshadowed by this popular rider's death.

It was soon discovered that the rule book did not allow for the loss of a rider in such sad circumstances, which prevented the Pirates from using guests. Injuries also claimed Malcolm Simmons and Eric Broadbelt, while Christer Sjosten rode in less than half of Poole's official fixtures, due to injuries or his conti-nental commitments. Gooddy, now 44 years old, was forced to double up with the Pirates and National League Crayford, but had such a remarkable season that he was named Rider of the Year at both tracks. Long-serving Pete Smith missed only two matches but retired at the end of the year, having completed fifteen seasons with Poole, his only club. Neil Middleditch was the only rider not to miss a match and qualified for both the British Final and the final of the European Under-21 Championship (predecessor of the World U21

Malcolm Simmons.

Championship), but was banned from taking part due to his progress in the senior World Championship.

The Pirates would repeat a hat-trick of tenth places finishes in 1978. It was to prove a year of consolidation with Malcolm Simmons again in supreme form and maintaining his 10-plus average, with which he also topped the British League scorers. Two new faces appeared in the line-up, American Mike Curoso and Andrzej Tkocz from Poland. Curoso moved south from Hull and took time to settle, so it was not until August that he began to show his true form. Tkocz suffered an early season shoulder injury so did not make his debut until the end of June, after which he showed enough promise for Poole to want him back.

Martin Yeates had his first full season in the British League. Danny Kennedy doubled up for the Pirates and Weymouth and proved a more than adequate scorer, but veteran Colin Gooddy announced his retirement after twice suffering serious back injuries. Poole Speedway also survived another major blow when the co-promoter and British Speedway Promoters' Association president, Mr Charles Foot, collapsed and died in a London hotel shortly before the Golden Jubilee World Final at Wembley. Mr Foot's passing would bring to a close the Knott family's connection with Poole, for midway through the 1979 season it was announced that multi-track promoter Reg Fearman and Pirates clerk of the course Terry Chandler would also be taking over the greyhound operation at Wimborne Road. At that stage of the season there were few changes that the new promotion could make to a side that were already destined to finish in the lower half of the table.

Simmons' supremacy was beginning to diminish. After a good start, a recurring leg injury first interrupted then ended his season and he was replaced in late October by Piotr Pyszny. Middleditch, Kennedy and Yeates all continued to make progress, the latter almost becoming a heat leader in the early part of the campaign. The major plus for the Pirates was the arrival of unknown American Ron Preston, who not only became a favourite with the crowd, but established himself as the second heat leader, overtaking Super Simmo in the home averages and to the surprise of many, won the European U21 Championship. The year ended in sadness when crowd pleaser Christer Sjosten crashed in a race at Brisbane in Australia at the beginning of December and died five days later.

The Pirates started the 1980 season with the addition to two former Exeter riders, Zimbabwean Peter Prinsloo and all action Czech, Vaclav Verner. The two ex-Falcons joined Malcolm Simmons, Ron Preston, Neil Middleditch, Danny Kennedy and £700 signing Kevin Bowen, in what looked like a solid line-up. The Pirates finished in the middle of the table but the season was blighted by simmering unrest between Chandler and Simmons. At one point Simmons was stripped of the captaincy, which was given to Middleditch. Matters came to a head in October when Chandler accused Simmons of deliberately allowing John Davis and Malcolm Holloway to win a race thus preventing team mate Ron Preston from winning the Sheba Pairs event at Wimborne Road. Simmons was sacked and immediately placed on the transfer list. The fans backed Simmo but to no avail, he never again donned the skull and cross-bones race jacket.

Of the rest Bowen never settled at British League level and was replaced by Australian John McNeill. Verner took time to settle in at Wimborne Road, but qualified for the World Final as reserve. Prinsloo immediately became third heat leader but Preston's season was hampered by a knee injury picked up at Poole while riding in the England *v.* USA test series. Kennedy overcame a pre-season broken ankle but failed to maintain his previous form. The test matches against the USA proved extremely popular, with the Americans winning 63-44 at Wimborne Road before going on to take the series 3-1.

Simmons joined Wimbledon for 1981 and was replaced at Poole by Scott Autrey who was later joined by John Davis from Reading. Locally based Davis had been Chandler's target for much of the previous year but he dismissed rumours of a £100,000 transfer offer. Poole's other big-money signing was American Scott Autrey, who was purchased from Swindon for £16,500. Autrey had previously shown his liking for the Poole track by breaking the track record during the Blue Riband indi-

vidual event for which he won a brand new car. Verner was prevented from returning by the Czech authorities, but Prinsloo, Kennedy and Middleditch all continued. Middleditch only missed one match but resigned the captaincy when his form dropped. A number of other riders were given opportunities, Aussie Malcolm Bedkober rode a dozen matches before poor equipment saw him replaced by Pete Ellams. Dane Claus Jensen rode thirteen matches but only scored 1 point thanks to the retirement of an opponent. Kevin Smith was purchased from Rye House for £10,000, and did so well that he was called up for England against the USA. Preston started the year but was forced to pull out before the British League campaign due to an ongoing knee injury. This allowed Poole to finally sign John Davis. However despite the amount of money that was spent on building the team the Pirates still only managed to finish ninth.

Poole were again allocated an England *v.* USA test match but this time England

Kevin Holden.

Eric Broadbelt outside Exeter's Mike Sampson.

won by two points, 55-53. 1982 would prove even more disappointing for the Pirates as despite their impressive line-up they would finish bottom of the British League for the first time. It was a huge disappointment as on paper the line-up was even stronger as Vaclav Verner returned to join Davis, Autrey, Prinsloo, Middleditch, Smith and Kennedy.

The season began encouragingly with home and away challenge victories over Reading. Swindon inflicted defeat in the first home League Cup match but the Pirates then rattled off six successive wins despite Kennedy's late return from Australia. Prinsloo was sidelined for seven weeks after a serious crash on Easter Monday and Ron Preston, who had missed most of the previous season through injury left to try his luck at Eastbourne. Even with Kennedy's return Poole's fortunes went into decline. Eastbourne forced a draw in the first British League fixture, Birmingham ousted the Pirates from the Knockout Cup and Belle Vue won the next League match. Of their twenty-eight British League matches Poole won just three, at home, against Coventry, Halifax and King's Lynn.

After a good start, Autrey's interest faded and he lost his enthusiasm after going out of the World Championship. Verner did not enjoy much success in Poole colours but reached the World Final in Los Angeles. Autrey, Prinsloo and Kennedy quit British speedway at the end of the year, while Smith ended the season nursing a broken arm. USA won the Poole test match 69-39 and by doing so clinched the series 3-2.

The arrival of former world champion Michael Lee in 1983 helped to lift the Pirates two places off the bottom of the table. Lee joined John Davis, Kevin Smith, Vaclav Verner, Neil Middleditch and another new signing Andy Campbell. He quickly put a couple of disappointing seasons behind him and achieved a 10-plus average, became a big favourite with the supporters and went on to finish third in the World Final at Norden in Germany. Davis still played his part, giving Lee solid support, and the Poole management, after tracking a number of different riders including Swedish ice champion Erik Stenland and Brian Jakobsen from Denmark, eventually brought over an up-and-coming American called Sam Ermolenko. Ermolenko only rode a handful of matches for Poole that summer but did enough to earn himself a team place for the following year.

The winter saw the departure of John Davis and Vaclav Verner while Andy Campbell returned to Exeter. Efforts were made to sign Erik Gundersen, Simon Wigg and Shawn Moran, but eventually Lee and Ermolenko headed a 1984 team which also now included Stan Bear, purchased from Weymouth, and Swedish newcomer Leif Wahlman.

Expectations were not high as the team was considered to be weaker than the previous season. But things took an unexpected course when Lee abandoned his bike on the starting line at King's Lynn following an engine failure. He was considered to have endangered the lives of his fellow competitors and was subsequently banned for five years. This heavy ban was probably the culmination of several other brushes with authority, but although it was later reduced on appeal Lee's career with Poole was effectively at an end.

The problems were again beginning to mount up for Poole as at the beginning of April Jakobsen fractured his skull in a second-half crash. Wahlman was loaned to Exeter in a bid to help him find his form only to be killed in a crash during the European Under-21 Final at King's Lynn.

Despite these difficulties the Pirates still managed to give a reasonable

Christer Sjosten.

145

'Super Simmo' in action.

account of themselves, at least at home, where they only lost four matches. The form of Sam Ermolenko was the silver lining, while Finn Thomson was talked out of retirement and after a couple of months took on the captaincy. Neil Middleditch marked his ten years as a Pirate with a well-deserved testimonial. Poole gave Germany's Gert Riss a try-out and he top-scored in the last of his four appearances, while American Bobby Ott also rode in a couple of late-season meetings.

But if the season had been problematic, the winter brought near disaster for the Pirates' fans when the promoting company, Poole Stadium Ltd went into liquidation in January 1985 with debts in excess of £200,000. Various local businessmen attempted takeovers but one by one these failed and it appeared Poole Speedway was finished. Fortunately at the eleventh hour Weymouth promoter Mervyn Stewkesbury stepped in and brought his National League Wildcats to Poole, complete with team manager Neil Street and coach Lew Coffin.

After 30 years in the top flight Poole reverted to a Second Division track, but as far as the fans were concerned National League was better than no speedway at all even though the new management switched the race night to Tuesday, Weymouth's traditional evening.

The new Poole Wildcats consisted in the main of former Weymouth riders namely ex-Pirate Martin Yeates, David Biles, Marcus Bisson and David Gibbs. An element of continuity was provided by Kevin Smith and Stan Bear, but sadly there was no place for Neil Middleditch or Sam Ermolenko. A late addition to the side was Guy Wilson who was transferred from defunct Boston.

After the many disappointments of recent seasons the switch to National League racing proved a major success and the Wildcats finished runners-up in the League championship. The title was effectively lost in the Wildcats' first match. Poole led by two points going into the final heat, but the Peterborough Panthers fought back to force a draw. Thereafter Poole won all their home matches and also picked up eight victories on the road but lost out to Ellesmere Port by a single point. Yeates and Bear were also runners-up in the National Pairs Championship but Poole lost to Wimbledon in the first round of the Knockout Cup.

1986 saw Steve Schofield rejoin the Wildcats. He had previously ridden for Stewkesbury at Weymouth but left to try his luck at Wolverhampton in the British League. Things had not worked out at Monmore Green and Schoie accepted the offer to replace the retired Stan Bear. He did so admirably and ended the season with a 10-plus average. Wilson was released while promising Ray Dole had also returned to Australia and would not be seen again on a British track. Schofield joined Yeates and Smith but with such a strong top end the Wildcats' management were forced to use their less experienced junior riders to complete the line-up. David Biles, David Gibbs, Jerseyman Marcus Bisson and Cornish newcomer Will James provided the bulk of support although Gordon Humphreys and Peter Read also had the occasional outing.

Poole maintained their unbeaten home National League record but away defeats at Birmingham, Middlesbrough, Rye House, Peterborough, Boston and Newcastle in the first three months of the season again cost them their chance of the championship. The Wildcats' hopes also received a further setback when Kevin Smith injured his leg while racing against Arena Essex in April and remained out of action until July. Although an away draw at Long Eaton and wins at Glasgow, Hackney, Canterbury, Edinburgh, Mildenhall and Exeter lifted Poole into second place, it was not quite enough to overhaul the eventual champions Eastbourne.

Arena Essex managed to put the Wildcats out of the Knockout Cup thanks to home and away wins early on, but Schofield finished runner-up to Paul Thorp in the NLRC.

After twice finishing as runners-up, hopes were high that Poole, once more the Pirates by popular demand, could go one better in 1987. Yeates, Schofield, Smith and Biles again gave Poole an extremely powerful top end, but after achieving a win over Peterborough in their first home League match and an away victory at Rye House, the Pirates suffered an injury crisis as Wayne Barrett, Will James and new signing Nigel Tremling were all hurt in the Peterborough match. Barrett and James returned to the side fairly quickly but Tremling was out for the season. Schofield was the next to be sidelined after being involved in a horrific crash at Exeter with Bruce Cribb.

Despite these losses, Poole managed close home wins over Long Eaton and Berwick, but went down to their first away defeat at Peterborough. Biles and Smith tangled at Berwick, resulting in Smith missing the following seven matches, and was soon joined in the casualty list for a second time by James. It would be July before all the top five lined up together again. Local junior Peter Read was given his opportunity in the team and Schofield and Biles were soon showing quality form, but the same could not be said of the reserves. Home form was maintained until Wimbledon ended Poole's almost three-year unbeaten run, but away from Wimborne Road the heat leaders lacked support and the Rye House win remained their sole success. As a result Poole had to be content with eighth place in the League table. David Biles gained an impressive fifth place in the National League Riders Championship, but the Pirates failed to feature in any of the other major events.

For 1988 major changes had to be made to the line-up following the retirement of both Martin Yeates and Kevin Smith. Schofield and Biles were now joined by Kevin Smart, two young Australians Craig Boyce and Tony Langdon, and a New Zealander, Gary Allan. Steve Bishop moved over from Exeter and two other new signings were Nigel Flatman and Robbie Fuller. The new line-up gelled well and a run of good results saw the Pirates once again end the season in second place.

During 1988 another young Australian had come to Britain to get acclimatised. 17-year-old Leigh Adams was recommended by both the team manager Neil Street and Phil Crump and, as he had not ridden in any National League matches, began the 1989 season on a 2-point average. This was just the boost Poole needed to lift them into the No.1 slot. Adams won his first League race at Ipswich and ended the match with paid 14 from six starts. He scored his first full maximum in the next match at Mildenhall and went on to end the season as second highest scorer to Boyce with a 9.21 average. That summer also saw Alun Rossiter join the Pirates along with another promising youngster Alistair Stevens. On the debit side, the popular Steve Schofield went on loan to Hackney, while David Biles had retired.

Despite a home defeat by Berwick and more rain-offs than any other team, the Pirates rounded off the year with a succession of away wins before beating Arena Essex 71-24 at Wimborne Road to clinch their first championship for 20 years in front of their own home fans. They also reached the final of the Knockout Cup but lost 109-83 to Berwick.

Such was Adams' meteoric rise that he went straight into the British League with Swindon in 1990, but not even that could stop the Pirates repeating their back to back championship of the 1960s. Other departures from Poole saw Kevin Smart sold to Long Eaton and Alistair Stevens recalled to Oxford. Into their places came Dane Tom Knudsen and Gary Chessell from Swindon, while Rod Colquhoun was signed from Peterborough. Craig Boyce, who had headed Adams in the averages the previous year, improved yet again, while skipper Alun Rossiter continue to motivate and cultivate the team spirit. This not only helped Poole to retain their title but also go one better and win the Knockout Cup by defeating Middlesbrough in the final.

The Pirates only lost five of their forty League matches. Boyce never scored less than double figures and even registered 17 paid 18 at Edinburgh in one of those rare defeats. By the end of the season, the Pirates were also giving rides to teenage prospect Mark Lemon and former mascot Justin Elkins. Boyce finished third in the National League Riders Championship and fulfilled his ambition by joining British League Oxford for 1991.

By now, promoter Meryvn Stewkesbury, who was also chairman of the National League promoters, was seeking new fields to conquer and wanted to take his team back into the top flight. During the winter he brokered a deal with the ailing British League to merge the two Leagues via a promotion relegation scheme. As a result of this move the Pirates moved back to the First Division, along with Wimbledon, Ipswich and Berwick. The move was the signal for Poole to sign Marvyn Cox and recall Steve Schofield from Hackney. Australian Mick Poole joined on loan from Peterborough while Alun Rossiter, Gary Allan and Tom Knudsen were all retained.

The 1986 Poole Wildcats. From left to right, back row: Will James, Wayne Barrett, Neil Street (manager), David Gibbs, Gordon Humphries. On bikes: Kevin Smith, Martin Yeates, Steve Schofield. Kneeling: David Biles, Marcus Bisson.

The 1991 season was to prove a struggle and although the Pirates started well by drawing on aggregate and forcing a rerun with Reading Racers in the Premiership their weaknesses soon became apparent. With three riders, Mick Poole, Knudsen and Langdon, coming back from serious injuries suffered the previous season the Pirates found life in the First Division tough going. They finished fifth out of seven in the early season Gold Cup competition, and in the League narrowly avoided relegation back to Division Two. After spending most of the summer at the bottom of the table a late flurry of success lifted Poole up three places to tenth.

In a late effort to strengthen the side, Poland's Slavomir Drabnik was given trials while Michael Lee began to take part in post-meeting practice sessions during which he unfortunately crashed and suffered a serious back injury. 16-year-old Jason Crump made a dozen appearances for the Poole reserve League team and twice rode for the Pirates during the autumn. Changes clearly needed to be made for 1992 and Stewkesbury and Ansell were not afraid to make them. Rossiter and Allan went out on loan to King's Lynn while Mick Poole returned to Peterborough. Into their places came Drabnik and Andy Phillips, a second stringer who has previously ridden for Wolverhampton and Coventry while to the delight of the Pirates' fans Craig Boyce returned after a disappointing season at Oxford.

Poole not only had a new team sponsor in JT Commercials, but also returned to their traditional Wednesday race night. Again the season started badly with four successive home defeats in the Gold Cup and an early exit from the Knockout Cup at the hands of Cradley. The promoters threatened more changes, but quickly realised that no suitable replacements were readily available. Eventually Drabnik was replaced by Sweden's Jorgen Johansson, while former Pirate Ali Stevens returned in place of Phillips.

Gradually Poole's fortunes turned and the Pirates began to claw their way up the table, becoming one of only four teams to beat eventual champions Reading on the way to third place. Poole also battled their way through to the final of the BSPA Cup where having overcome Reading 50-40 in the first leg, they lost 62-38 at Smallmead.

Throughout the season the uncertain future of Poole stadium loomed over the Pirates' management, but this was resolved when the owners' company went into liquidation and the town council took over on a temporary basis. Hopes for the Pirates' continuing progress were severely hit when Marvyn Cox refused to accept the new pay scale introduced for 1993 and instead moved abroad and took out a German licence. Leigh Adams, who had once again become a Poole asset when Stewkesbury took over relegated Swindon, also declined to ride at Wimborne Road and he eventually joined Arena Essex.

The Poole management expected and anticipated help from the BSPA, and although a dispensation to use a guest was initially granted, it would later be rescinded. Boyce and Schofield carried the team, with help from new Norwegian signing Lars Gunnestad, and towards the end of the campaign veteran American John 'Cowboy' Cook stepped in to fill the No.1 slot. Ray Morton was signed on loan, but was injured in the last month of the season, while Scott Swain was purchased from Eastbourne as a reserve. Once again it was a difficult year for the Pirates who finished tenth out of eleven with little to show for their efforts. For fans with a long memory it had been reminiscent of the late sixties, but it was hoped that 1994 would bring a return to the glory days.

Improvements to the team cost nothing as the Pirates' line-up only saw the addition of two Second Division riders from sister club Swindon – Jason Crump and Steve Masters. Crump had started out at Peterborough in 1992, then switched to Swindon the following year where he topped the Second Division averages. Also making another move from Blunsden was Alun Rossiter, who having been left out of Swindon's team, found that his average fitted Poole's reserve requirements. Steve Schofield, Lars Gunnestad and Jorgan Johansson were retained, but for a while, Boyce's return was uncertain following his public criticism of the management the previous season. Elkins was named as the other reserve and replaced Scott Swain.

Early setbacks came when Johansson was injured in a practice session at Swindon and Crump suffered concussion while racing in Poland. Undeterred he bounced back

Craig Boyce.

to score a maximum in Poole's second match, an away win at Belle Vue, but during April the Pirates were dumped out of the Knockout Cup by King's Lynn.

In June Gunnestad scored his first 15-point maximum in a home victory over Eastbourne, and a third Swindon rider, Steve Masters, arrived to replace Elkins. By this stage of the season the Pirates were winning consistently at home, had won six away matches and also qualified for the Four Team Championship final at Peterborough. King's Lynn had become Poole's main rivals for the championship, and a timely 71-25 victory over the Knights at Wimborne Road now put Poole in the driving seat. A further five League victories followed, including a 58-36 success at Bradford, and the Pirates were once again champions. Gunnestad unfortunately injured his knee in the Norwegian Championship which put him out for the remainder of the season but Poole were refused permission to replace him with Long Eaton's Jan Staechman as the 31 August transfer deadline had been passed. The season ended on a controversial note when the final match at Eastbourne was rained off. When it proved impossible to find a restaging date the match was awarded to Poole 86-0!

On the individual front, Schofield finished third in the British Final of the World Championship. Crump finished third in the World Under-21 Final and also, along with team mate Craig Boyce, qualified for his first individual World Final at Vojens in Denmark. He managed to win his first race, but could not match Boyce who finished an excellent third in the three-man run off of what was to be the last one-off world finals.

Concerns over the long term future of speedway in Poole ended when a new 10-year lease was agreed with Bliston Developments. Poole Town FC also announced that they would be quitting the stadium which allowed the Pirates' management to start making plans to widen the speedway track. 1995 also saw the formation of a new combined Premier League. The original intention was to limit each team to one First Division rider with an average in excess of 8 points. Poole were given special dispen-

Leigh Adams.

sation to use Steve Schofield but still had three riders, Jason Crump, Craig Boyce and Lars Gunnestad who boasted averages in excess of the agreed limit. Stewkesbury successfully fought to keep his riders, and his attitude along with that of other former First Division promoters contributed to the failure of the Premier League to achieve its full potential. It certainly prevented the Second Division clubs from signing the star riders that would have made them competitive at this level.

Boyce went out on loan to Swindon after failing to agree terms with the Poole management, but Crump, who had earlier requested a transfer to Blunsdon, agreed to stay along with Schofield, Gunnestad, Rossiter and Masters. Jorgen Johansson stayed in Sweden, so Jason Bunyan contested the reserve slots with local lads, Justin Elkins and Martin Willis.

Alun Rossiter.

The Pirates opened the season with an away win at Coventry, but lost the Premiership to Eastbourne. Gunnestad fractured a scaphoid in the home match against Exeter on Good Friday. The injury would keep him out for six weeks, while Schofield broke three bones in his foot at Oxford and was sidelined until June. Kelvin Tatum was signed as a short-term replacement, but ten out of twelve matches had been lost. Crump later injured his wrist at Wolverhampton, but was able to continue riding. Although the Pirates suffered a number of further defeats they eventually finished twelfth out of twenty-one.

Gunnestad had quickly found his form and broke the Poole track record four times. As a result of his increased success the Norwegian star was named as a wild card for the Swedish Grand Prix. However, a protest by Sweden and Peter Karlsson saw him switched to the Danish GP at Vojens instead. In August, Crump finally won the World Under-21 Championship and as champion appeared at the British GP at Hackney, where he narrowly failed to make the A final. Shortly before this meeting Pirates' team manager, Neil Street, was rushed home from Poland with a life-threatening abscess on his liver as a result of which he spent several months recovering in hospital. During the winter tests were made on the foundations of the stadium with a view to a major redevelopment of the facilities; once again the Pirates' future was put in jeopardy as the town council and the potential developers could not reach agreement.

Jason Crump's request for a transfer was finally granted and 1996 saw him move to Peterborough, while Craig Boyce was recalled from Swindon to replace him. Gunnestad and Schofield continued as heat leaders and two new faces, Magnus Zetterstom and Marcus Andersson, arrived from Sweden. There was no room for the ever-popular Rossiter, who joined Crump at Peterborough, while Steve Masters returned to Swindon. Jason Bunyan was given a further opportunity at reserve along with Norway's Inger Hvarstad, who had appeared in half a dozen matches the previous season.

During the winter the promotion had finally been able to go ahead with their plans to revamp the track following the departure of greyhounds and football. The old narrow circuit was replaced by a new 300m FIM standard circuit which promised better racing, but the Pirates' opening match, against Exeter on Good Friday, certainly did not go as expected. Schofield crashed into Exeter's Paul Fry in his first race, and the Falcons went on to achieve their first away win for four years. Worse was to follow when Marcus Andersson fell during an after-match practice and damaged his knee ligaments. Although Poole drew at Exeter on Easter Monday, Zetterstrom crashed after scoring an impressive 5 points in his first two races and suffered back injuries. Two days later Bunyan also hurt his back and Lee Richardson was brought from Reading to replace him. Andersson quickly recovered from his injuries but Tony Langdon was flown in from Australia to strengthen the team, arriving just in time to help Poole gain their first League win against Belle Vue.

In May the Pirates won the first leg of their Knockout Cup tie at Exeter (51-46) and looked certain to go through. The return leg 48 hours later was rained off and delayed until late June when Exeter achieved another shock win at Wimborne Road and claimed aggregate victory. Langdon finished sixth in the Overseas Final but was then disqualified due to a tyre dispute. He was so upset by this development that shortly afterwards he returned home to Australia. Christer Johnsson came in to replace the injured Zetterstrom, but was replaced by Jorgen Johansson who rode a handful of matches. Poole now languished at the bottom of the table but after achieving an away win at Long Eaton managed to avoid the wooden spoon by successfully climbing five slots up the League to finish fourteenth. The home match against Swindon on 17 July had to be abandoned when the safety fence could not be repaired in time following an alarming crash involving Gunnestad and Robins' Jarno Kososen. As twelve heats had been raced the result stood and Swindon won 44-34. Bunyan recovered from his back injury but was disappointed to learn that Poole preferred to keep his replacement Lee Richardson, who was being advised by John Davis. Zetterstrom, having recovered from his injury, was able to rejoin the team in September.

Poole staged an England *v.* Australia test match which resulted in a 48-48 draw while Gunnestad won the prestigious Blue Riband individual contest. Sadly Boyce lost his place in the World Championship after scoring just 2 points in the Grand Prix Challenge.

Despite having finished in the bottom half of the table for two years it was clear that Poole would compete in the newly formed Elite League when big League split again in 1997. The new points limit and six-man teams allowed the Pirates to put together a team comprising mainly their own assets. Marvyn Cox returned after four years away from Wimborne Road while Australian Mark Lemon was set for his first full season with his parent club. Craig Boyce, Lars Gunnestad and Steve Schofield again formed the spearhead of the side while Ipswich loanee and British Under-21 champion Savalas Clouting completed the line-up.

The season started spectacularly with home and away Knockout Cup wins over King's Lynn and Peterborough. Ipswich were beaten at Wimborne Road and Eastbourne thrashed 73-17 following a notorious row over alleged tyre tampering. But what looked like being a successful year quickly turned sour when first Bradford inflicted a 16-point home defeat and then a heath fire beside the M3 motorway near Camberley seriously delayed Schofield and Clouting and in their absence arch-rivals Eastbourne returned to Poole and won.

Lars Gunnerstad, Bo Hadek, Jason Crump and Mark Loram come off the start at Poole, Good Friday 1995.

Jason Crump and Mark Loram.

Despite again being at the foot of the League table Poole managed to beat Coventry and reach the final of the Speedway Star Knockout Cup. Another boost came when the Pirates went north to Bradford, where the Dukes were well on course for the League championship, and won by 18 points, only to be beaten at home a few days later by Peterborough. To add to Poole's difficulties Boyce broke his wrist, and Gunnerstad damaged shoulder ligaments. Efforts were made to sign Tony Rickardsson but he eventually rejoined Ipswich, a move that allowed Ben Howe to sign for the Pirates.

In August Schofield, who earlier in the season had become Poole's highest-ever scorer was dramatically axed along with Cox. Reading's popular Italian Armando Castagna was brought in as a replacement but never really got going after such a late start, and asked to be released. Hopes of Knockout Cup glory also disappeared when Eastbourne won the first leg of the final in Dorset and before clinching the cup back home at Arlington. Having finished bottom of the Elite League the Poole season closed with a special test match between England and the USA in memory of America's English team manager, John Scott, who had died earlier in the season. England won 46-44.

Having finished bottom of the Elite League the previous year, the Poole management knew that they had to pull their socks up for 1998. The revamped Wimborne Road track had been granted an FIM licence, while the stadium now also boasted a smart restaurant complex. Thanks to the new FIM status Poole was allocated the

Overseas Final and at one point was also in the running to stage the British Grand Prix. The Pirates' main team sponsor, JT Commercials, pulled out after six seasons and was replaced by Hair Arena.

During the winter unsuccessful attempts were made to sign both Mark Loram and Garry Stead who had both previously ridden for recently closed Bradford. Instead Ryan Sullivan arrived on loan from Peterborough while Magnus Zetterstrom returned once more to join the '97 regulars, Marvyn Cox, Lars Gunnestad, Craig Boyce and Mark Lemon.

Sadly Poole's fortunes did not greatly improve as far as either results or weather were concerned, as no fewer than nine meetings were rained off. Sullivan had the misfortune to be injured in his very first race and, in May, Cox sustained a badly fractured thigh when his footrest caught in the fence and he was thrown over the handlebars. Changes were again made in mid-season as once more the Pirates struggled. Rider replacement was initially used for Cox but as both Boyce and Gunnerstad were finding points hard to come by Kelvin Tatum was again signed as a short-term replacement. 1992 world champion Gary Havelock, unhappy at Eastbourne, accepted an offer to join the Pirates and made an immediate impression both on the track and in the pits. Havelock's arrival coincided with the departure of Zetterstrom who had dropped to reserve, and eventually Poole managed to avoid a second wooden spoon by finishing eighth.

Clearly Poole needed to return to winning ways but few had anticipated a change of management was in the offing. Mervyn Stewkesbury, disillusioned with the way speedway was being run and frustrated at not being able to finalise a long term lease on the stadium sold his 100 per cent holding to two local businessmen, Matt Ford of Hair Arena, Poole's main sponsor, and Mike Golding of McM Cars. They pledged to bring the glory days back to Wimborne Road and had already begun to made wholesale team changes before their takeover was made public. Craig Boyce, so long the main man at Wimborne Road was the first to go. Mark Loram was finally signed on loan from Exeter while Gary Havelock became a permanent Poole asset. They were joined by Scott Nicholls who wanted a change from Ipswich while Pirates' 1998 Rider of the Year Magnus 'Zorro' Zetterstrom was set to return. At this stage the takeover was made public along with the signing of Slovenian Matej Ferjan who had failed to settle at Belle Vue the previous year. The long awaited signing of up and coming star Lee Richardson from Premier League Reading was finally confirmed and the new line-up was completed by local boy Martin Willis. The team also had a new main sponsor in L&G Specialist Micro Oils, distributors of ZX1, and thus Poole became the ZX1 Pirates. Their long-serving team manager Neil Street was replaced by the popular former Pirate Neil Middleditch while co-promoter Pete Ansell agreed to stay on in an advisory capacity.

The new-look Pirates started the 1999 season with home and away Craven Shield wins over Eastbourne and a draw at Belle Vue. Although they lost at home to Oxford, an away win at Ipswich, by a single point, earned them a place in the semi-finals.

The Elite League also began with home and away successes against the Eagles. The Pirates remained unbeaten at home, and further away triumphs at Wolverhampton and Oxford put Poole in contention for the League championship. That summer Sky TV had begun their regular weekly coverage of the Elite League and the campaign climaxed on Wednesday 30 September with simultaneous televised matches between Peterborough and Belle Vue, and King's Lynn and Poole. The Pirates needed to win at Saddlebow Road to snatch the title from the Panthers. But while Peterborough comfortably beat the Aces forty miles up the road Poole went into the final race at King's Lynn needing a 4-2 to be champions. Sadly Loram and Havelock were unable to overcome Tony Rickardsson and Leigh Adams, and the anguish and disappointment on Middlo's face shown in close-up on TV said it all.

Peterborough also ended Poole's hopes of Craven Shield glory by winning the much-delayed semi-final and then rubbed salt into the wounds by beating the Pirates again in the final of the Speedway Star Knockout Cup. Nevertheless it was a good season for Poole, crowds had flocked to see the revitalised Pirates and Loram had not only won the Swedish GP as a wild card but successfully reclaimed his regular World Championship place at the Grand Prix Challenge at Lonigo in Italy. Sadly Havvy was not so successful and failed to qualify at Lonigo, but Richardson had showed his worth by becoming the World Under-21 champion.

Richardson would be missing from the Pirates line-up in 2000 having decided that he wanted to ride for Coventry instead. Zetterstrom was also ruled out after doubts were expressed regarding his fitness after seriously fracturing a leg towards the end of the '99 campaign. Ferjan returned to Belle Vue and into the Poole team came Australian Craig Watson from Newport. The ever popular Lars Gunnerstad was recalled and Justin Elkins given another opportunity at reserve.

Having had more time to plan their team Ford and Golding were quietly confident that the new line-up was good enough to go one step further than in 1999. It was view shared by several riders and pundits. Alas things began to go wrong almost immediately. The second home match saw new Aussie Craig Watson collide with Eastbourne's David Norris on the back straight as a result of which he broke five bones in his arm and elbow. The Eagles went on to win the match and, apart from a handful of appearances much later in the summer, Watson's season was already over. Elkins struggled at reserve and after fourteen matches was replaced by the evergreen Alun Rossiter.

The 2000 campaign proved to be a mid-table season for the Pirates as they dropped to fifth place in the Elite League. Eastbourne, Coventry, Wolverhampton and King's Lynn all won at Wimborne Road while Belle Vue and Oxford drew. Away from home, Poole won at Oxford, Peterborough, Coventry and twice at Belle Vue. They also drew at Ipswich. Having beaten Oxford in the Knockout Cup the Pirates went out to Peterborough in the second round but managed to finish as runners-up in the Craven Shield. The greatest success by far was the impressive way in which the management continued to increase attendances on a regular basis. One of the biggest crowds turned out to welcome Mark Loram back after he had become the first Poole rider to win the World Championship in September. That month also saw Barry Briggs join forces with the Pirates' promotion to stage one of his popular Golden Greats events which featured many former riders including five times world champion Ove Fundin.

A 1996 programme cover.

Steve Schofield chats to Paul Fry.

To many long-standing Poole fans the highlight of the evening came when the legendary Brian 'Nipper' Crutcher was persuaded back onto a bike for the first time since 1961 and rode a couple of emotional laps.

During the winter Ford and Golding failed to agree a new deal with Mark Loram who moved to Peterborough, while Scott Nicholls was recalled by Ipswich. The Pirates faced a major rebuild for 2001 as Alun Rossiter and Emil Lindqvist were both released. Having lost one world champion in Loram the promoters wasted no time in signing another, Tony Rickardsson. Pole Greg Walasek, who had spent a month with Poole towards the end of the previous summer, was given a contract while two relatively unknown continental youngsters, Krzysztof Cegielski from Poland and the Dane Hans Andersen were also signed Havelock, Gunnerstad and Watson were all retained and together the new look team rattled off nine wins from their first ten challenge, League and Knockout Cup matches.

Cegielski and Andersen quickly proved their worth and once again the Pirates became serious challengers for the Elite League championship even though Gunnerstad was soon sidelined with a broken leg. Shortly afterwards Andersen fractured his thigh and then Walasek missed several weeks with a broken wrist. During this run of injuries the Pirates lost at home to Ipswich after initially holding a

16-point lead. It would prove to be a crucial result for Poole who eventually missed out to Oxford in the championship race. For the second time in three years the Pirates had lost the title by a single point.

Bogey club Ipswich also ended Poole's hopes of Knockout Cup glory in the first round, but the Pirates eventually lifted some silverware when they defeated Wolverhampton and Peterborough in the three-legged final of the Craven Shield. And for the second year running the Wimborne Road faithful turned out in their thousands to welcome home the world champion, this time the ultra professional Rickardsson, who like that Pirates' icon of the seventies Malcolm Simmons before him, had already proved himself virtually unbeatable around the Poole track all summer.

The ever-popular Magnus Zetterstrom had again reappeared to cover for Andersen during the injury crisis and the Poole management, always with an eye to the future, had signed David Ruud, the exciting Swedish prospect.

Rickardsson's services were retained for 2002 but unfortunately due to the controversial new ruling which prohibited teams tracking more than one Grand Prix rider there was no place for the extremely popular Cegielski. Havelock continued as skipper along with Hans Andersen, who had recovered from his broken thigh, and Greg Walasek. Ruud wanted another season in Sweden before coming to Britain full-time, so Dane Bjerne Pedersen was signed from Newcastle while two more young Poles, Mariusz Staszewski and Tomasz Chrzanowski joined the Pirates.

Poole's season began successfully with a win at King's Lynn but Walasek became an early injury victim when he fractured his ankle. Co promoter Matt Ford wasted no time in recalling Magnus 'Zorro' Zetterstrom to the Poole line-up and with Andersen struggling to recapture his old form it looked as though the popular Swede was back for the season. But by the time Walasek was fit again Andersen was scoring steadily again and disappointed Zorro joined Peterborough on loan.

To ensure that Sky TV viewers would witness the climax of the Elite League championship (Oxford having clinched the title the previous summer in a non-televised match) a new play-off system had been devised whereby the team that topped the table at the completion of the fixtures would go straight to the final where they would be joined by the winners of a knockout round contested by the next four teams. Eastbourne and Wolverhampton set the early pace with Poole targeting third place which would give them a home draw in the play offs. With twelve successive home League victories to their credit the Pirates were comfortably on course to qualify until a sequence of injuries threatened to ruin their chances. Walasek fractured his thigh spectacularly in a televised match against Wolverhampton in which the Wolves ended Poole's unbeaten run. The August bank holiday saw Havelock break his arm in the first of two home matches against King's Lynn. In the second match of the evening guest Alun Rossiter was also involved in a crash as a result of which he seriously damaged his knee ligaments. Lars Gunnerstad and Henka Gustaffsson were drafted in to fill the gaps but Coventry snatched a late 47-43 victory at Wimborne Road. This gave the Bees a home advantage over the Pirates when the two teams met the following week in the quarter-final of the play offs. Although Rickardsson won his first

A 1999 programme cover.

three races he was forced to withdraw due to illness. Without him Poole were unable to wipe out Coventry's early 12-point lead and eventually lost 59-31.

The Pirates did not end the season empty-handed as they successfully retained the Craven Shield, beating Coventry and Peterborough in the three-legged final. Rickardsson had also dominated the Grand Prix series and claimed the title for the fifth time enabling the Pirates' management to parade the new world champion at Wimborne Road for the third successive season.

Tony Rickardsson was virtually unbeatable at Poole. He claimed the biggest cash prize ever offered in Britain – £7,500 – when he won Poole's special meeting to celebrate the Queen's Golden Jubilee, and also won the Elite League Riders Championship, which was being staged for the first time at the Dorset track. Poole also hosted a test match between Team GB and Sweden which the Swedes won 48-42, and the second qualifying round of the Speedway World Cup. This also proved a convincing victory for Sweden with Rickardsson storming to a 15-point maximum.

While the Elite League championship may have again eluded the Pirates it was yet another memorable season at Poole and once again the promotion's efforts had continued to attract the best crowds in the country.

RINGWOOD

Ringwood is generally better known as a training track rather than a League venue, but it was also the home of a successful Southern Area League team in the mid-1950s. The track was situated in the picturesque wooded setting of Matchams Park south of the A31 on the outskirts of Bournemouth in Hampshire.

The original speedway track was located at the rear of the existing stadium and operated between 1937 and 1939. Records show that in 1938 Ringwood staged a match against Holbeach in which 'Crasher' Warren rode unbeaten for the visitors. Holbeach returned the following season and on 18 June beat Ringwood (who on that occasion rode as Bournemouth) 62-40.

A Ringwood team also rode at Wrougham Speedway in Wiltshire on Sunday 19 June 1938 as part of a Mountain Grass-track race meeting organised by the Swindon Works Motor Club (racing section); the 'Works' being the Great Western Railway. Wroughton won the nine-heat match 35-19, and were led by Bristol speedway rider Roger Wise. Ringwood included Herbie Hayden, Bingley Cree and Tom Crutcher.

In the aftermath of the Second World War Ringwood staged open meetings, and practice sessions in 1946 and 1947. In 1950 John Crutcher took over the running of the track. He brought in the former Poole track curator Alf Elliott, who laid a new 385-yard red shale circuit which incorporated a concrete starting area complete with an up-to-date electric starting gate. That year the track was used primarily for training, and it was at the practice session held on Boxing Day that the future England international and Poole legend Brian Crutcher made his first appearance on a speedway track. Crutcher would become the greatest of all the riders who learnt their trade at Ringwood.

The track at Matchams Park also staged speedway car racing. An advertisement in the *Bournemouth Echo* referred to a meeting on 27 August in which a 'team composed of well-known local racing men will challenge teams from Northampton and Brighton in a three cornered match'.

The first race meeting to be held was the St Leonard's Novices Championship. It took place on 5 May 1951 and was won by Ron Goulding. The meeting took its title from the notice board at the tree-lined entrance to Matchams Park which proclaimed 'St Leonard's Training Track'. That summer the track length was reduced to 375 yards and training sessions continued until 1954 with the public actively encouraged to attend. A crowd of nearly 2,000 watched the first fortnightly meeting in July 1952 and saw the Discoveries beat the Future Stars 42-38.

It was not only local riders who used the Ringwood training facilities. The Falkoping Motor Klubb from Sweden approached John Crutcher asking if they could practise there prior to the Swedish season. Agreement was reached and the Swedes spent three days at the track.

In September Southampton riders took part in a challenge involving the trainees. Saints' Bert Croucher led the victorious Reds who beat the Blues 50-34.

The following month Denis Hayles' team beat the Jimmy Coughlan team 42-40. Coughlan broke the track record in the first heat with a time of 74.2 seconds, the previous record time 75 seconds having been set by Hayles. Maurie Mattingley then reduced it to 74 seconds in heat 5, scored maximum points in the match, and went on to win the top-scorers' race from Coughlan.

One of the regular riders at Ringwood was Harold Carder but in 1954 he quit so that he could become the promoter of the newly named Ringwood Turfs which he entered in the Southern Area League. This newly formed League was intended as a junior competition for training tracks most of which operated on Sunday afternoons and was made up of Aldershot, the California Poppies (Reading), Brafield (Northampton), Eastbourne and Rye House as well as Ringwood. The first match, at Matchams Park on 4 April, saw Ringwood beat Aldershot 61-22 in a challenge. The Turfs' Alby Golden clocked the fastest time at the track so far: 73.2 seconds. A fortnight later Ringwood defeated the Brafield Flying Foxes 51-24 in a second challenge. This time it was Ernie Lessiter who impressed for the home side with a 12-point maximum before going on to win all his second-half races.

When the League got under way in May the Turfs lost 53-30 at Aldershot, but scored their first away win at Eastbourne on 23 May where they beat the Eagles 59-25. Golden led the scorers with a 12-point maximum closely followed by Merv Hannam on 11 and Lessiter with 10.

A second victory was achieved the following weekend when California were beaten 46-38 at Matchams. Lessiter scored another maximum and also broke the track record with a time of 72.2 seconds. Sunday afternoon speedway at Ringwood became increasingly popular and the Turfs were soon attracting big crowds.

The next home match saw the Turfs beaten 48-35 by Brafield on a wet track. The Flying Foxes took two 5-1 maximums from the first three races and never looked back. Lessiter, Hanham and Golden scored all but 9 of the Turfs' total.

July began with a 47-37 home win over California in a match that had plenty of incident. The Turfs' Jack Hillard was injured in an early race while later in the match Tommy Worrall, who had been transferred to Ringwood from Rye House, collided with Gil Goldfinch. Goldfinch needed nineteen stitches in his leg after it was trapped against the engine by his bent footrest.

The return at California – the track was situated at Longmoor near Woking – on Sunday 18 July saw Ringwood defeated 45-39 but clearly Goldfinch made a quick recovery as he scored 10 points. Lessiter continued his successful run with another maximum but the defeat was a setback to the Turfs' League title aspirations.

Ringwood kept their hopes alive with an impressive 50-33 win over top-of-the-table Rye House. The Turfs maintained their championship challenge with a solid 50-20 home win over Eastbourne with Lessiter again on maximum form. This result gave Ringwood every encouragement for their away match at Arlington a week later, but without Lessiter and Golden, who failed to score after his clutch disintegrated and hit him in the face, the Turfs lost 41-37 and their title hopes were gone.

Ringwood went on to beat Rye House and Brafield at home but lost away at both tracks. The Turfs finished the season in third place two points behind champions Rye

House. Both second-place California and Ringwood finished on 18 points but the Poppies claimed runners-up spot thanks to superior race points.

The Turfs enjoyed more success on the individual front when Alby Golden and Ernie Lessiter tied for first place in the League Riders Championship at Rye House. Golden narrowly won the run off and as a result earned himself a contract with Southampton for the following season.

Practice at Matchams started early in 1955 and in March Brian Crutcher, now with Wembley Lions, had a pre-season run out with the novices. There was a good turn-out of both fans and riders, among whom were Bristol junior Cliff Cox and Glyn Chandler. Chandler was offered a team place with the Turfs and readily accepted.

With Lessiter and Golden having joined Southampton the Ringwood team which lost 50-34 in a challenge match at Brafield looked very different to the previous season's line-up. The new look Turfs included Merv Hannam, Tom Reader, Glyn Chandler, B. Hayes, Ted Lewis, Jerry Bridson, Tony Worrall, G. Meredith and Gordon Short.

A second defeat followed at Rye House where Ringwood were decisively beaten 57-24. Experienced Mike Tams was included in the Turfs' line up but failed to make an impression and was later banned from riding at this level.

Ringwood's opening match again Rye House was called off due to rain and a third League defeat followed at California. The Poppies won 47-37 the following week at Matchams. The Turfs problems began when Gordon Richards blew his motor first time out and took no further part in the meeting. However the now declining number of Ringwood fans were able draw some satisfaction from Chandler's Silver Sash victory over Peter Mould.

The Turfs finally achieved a win on 22 May when they beat Eastbourne 53-27. Hannam was top scorer with 12 while Chandler bagged 11 and defended the Silver Sash against Wally Wilson. The match produced some good racing but the crowds had declined. Stock racing was now all the rage and the victory over Eastbourne would be the Turfs' last home appearance. It was announced that work needed to be done on the track and future home matches would be raced at Rye House. The track would in fact be tarmacked for the stock cars at a cost of £2,000.

The final away matches took place at Rye House and Brafield. The Turfs lost 61-22 at Hoddesdon where several Ringwood riders crashed including Glyn Chandler who was subsequently unable to defend his Silver Sash. Vic Ridgeon and Mike Broadbanks had both scored 12-point maximums, but the Sash went to Ridgeon who clocked the faster time. This decision did not please the crowd, who wanted a race-off.

The Turfs' final match took place at Brafield on Sunday 26 June. Hannam and Gridson, along with promoter-rider Harold Carder had been snapped up by struggling Eastbourne so at the Northamptonshire track the Ringwood team included Brian Elliott.

Speedway did not return to Matchams Park until 1970 when Mike Broadbanks ran training schools on a new track built inside the stock car circuit. Regular training sessions continued until 1973 when Russell Foot won the final meeting, the open training school championship, with a 15-point maximum. Hopes of speedway continuing were dashed the following year by plans to redevelop the stadium.

The bikes were not heard again at Ringwood until the late '80s. Rumours were circulating regarding the future of speedway at Poole Stadium and the Pirates promoters were believed to have approached the Matchams Park management regarding a possible move. In the end the Pirates remained at Wimborne Road but representatives from Poole rebuilt the training track and Kevin Smart was the first rider to use it in July 1988. Sessions were held there during 1989 and 1990 including one run by Jeremy Doncaster. The last training session is thought to have taken place on 7 February 1993.

By this time a mini long-track had also been built around the outside of the stock car track and the first meeting was held on 23 June 1988. Regular events took place under the auspices of a local motorcycle club.

The 1993 season was set to open on Saturday 13 March with a meeting which included solos, and sidecar challenge match between speedway and grasstrack. The solo entry was headed by Vaclav Verner, David Steen, Ben Howe and Justin Elkins. Sadly no races took place as tragically in the pre-meeting practice session a sidecar outfit driven by Andy Glennie collided with the unique inside safety fence, which shielded the stock car fence, and in the ensuing accident his passenger Peter Lane was killed. Glennie sustained multiple injuries but no other competitors were involved. The meeting was immediately cancelled and no further racing has taken place on the mini long-track.

PART V

WEYMOUTH

WEYMOUTH

The first reports linking speedway with the Dorset seaside resort of Weymouth appeared in 1949 when Mr J.E. Crutcher, the former Poole manager, revealed that he planned to open a track in the town. These plans centred around a site on Wyke Regis Road, but did not materialise. In May 1951, J.W. Coates, his wife and S.F. Crew were reported to be seeking the purchase of seventeen acres of land on another site with the intention of building a speedway and sports stadium. This project also apparently ran into trouble when at a hearing at Winchester Assizes the prospective promoters failed to gain possession of the site. Eighteen months later it was announced that stadium building would start in the autumn of 1953 when the land became available, but it was not until the spring of 1954 that work finally began on yet another site, a farm at Radipole Lane.

The promoting company, Wessex Stadiums Ltd, consisted of Mr Coates and R. Barzilay who engaged the highly experienced Bill Dutton as manager. The winter freeze delayed construction work by a further two weeks but Dutton lost no time in assembling his team, hopeful that the SCB would grant the new track League status.

The new track measured 379 yards, and eventually opened on Wednesday 4 August with an international challenge between Young England and Young Overseas, prior to which the reigning world champion, Freddie Williams, carried out the official opening ceremony. A reputed 17,000 people turned up to see Young England win 48-35. Dick Bradley won the first-ever race in the fastest time of night, 71.8 seconds.

The Weymouth team were nicknamed the Scorchers and wore a blue race jacket with a smiling yellow sun emblazoned on the front. Due to their later start the Scorchers were unable to compete in the Southern League as had been originally intended, so instead they raced a series of challenge matches against other West Country teams. The first of these was against Southampton when the Weymouth line-up included Exeter's Don Hardy and Goog Hoskin as guests. Hoskin won the opening race while Hardy scored Weymouth's first 12-point maximum as the Scorchers achieved their initial victory, 45-39. The regular team members included Chum Taylor, Gerald Pugh, Bert Clarke, Jack Mountford, Jack Cunningham and Harry Serrier.

The Scorchers lost to Oxford, but the following Tuesday, 24 August, Exeter were beaten 43-41 in a last heat decider. Two defeats, by the Rayleigh Rockets and a powerful West of England Select followed, but the last match of that short season saw Weymouth round off with a convincing victory over Swindon.

Heartened by their successful start, the Weymouth management applied to join the newly enlarged Second Division. The Scorchers' application was accepted at a promoters' meeting on Sunday 13 March 1955, with Friday as their chosen race night. The proposed starting line-up included Danny Dunton, Frankie Johnston, Ken Adams, Eddie Lack, Ernie Lessiter and Gerald Pugh.

The Scorchers made another successful start beating Exeter 51-44 at Radipole Lane on Good Friday. Ernie Brecknell top scored with 10 points while reserve Ernie Lessiter

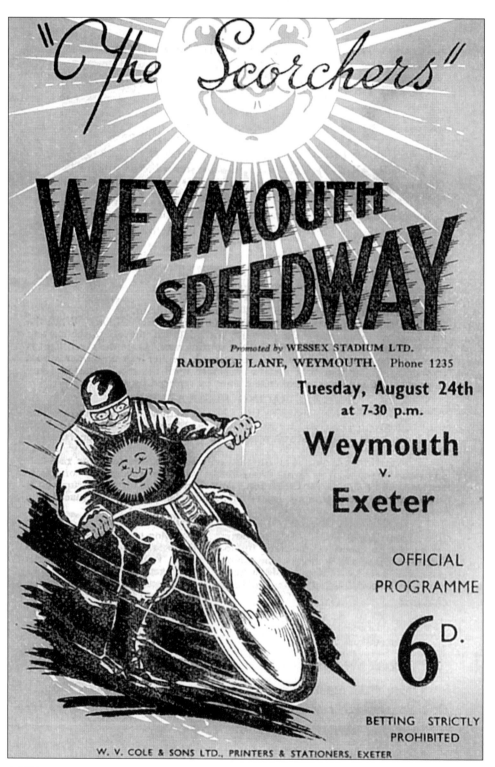

A 1954 programme cover.

began with two race wins. Sadly the euphoria would not last long as this was the Scorchers' only League victory. On 11 April Weymouth travelled to Ipswich and lost 62-34. Back at Radipole Lane Coventry won 59-37 with Tommy Miller scoring a 15-point maximum while Jim Lightfoot set a new track record, 70.6 seconds.

The Scorchers then faced Southampton Saints home and away in the National Trophy. In the first leg at Banister Court, the Scorchers were thrashed 70-38, and four days later back in Dorset went down 59-49. Two further heavy defeats followed, Weymouth losing 62-34 at Oxford, then 60-36 to Swindon at Radipole Lane.

Poole Pirates made their first appearance at Weymouth on 6 May and won 56-40. The meeting was not without incident as a big argument developed between Bill Dutton and Mr W.E. Potter, the ACU steward, regarding unsatisfactory starts. Due to their early exit from the National Trophy the Scorchers had no meeting the following week but on 20 May they lost at home to Rayleigh.

Three days later it was announced that the track had closed due to poor results and declining attendances. The decision was regarded by many as premature given that the main holiday season in the seaside town was about to begin, but clearly the promoters were already facing serious financial difficulties.

With speedway gone the stadium was used for stock car racing until the late fifties and as well as speedway training sessions. On Friday 20 July 1962, television cameraman and former Aldershot promoter John Pilblad relaunched speedway with an individual event, the Wessex Championship, run over sixteen heats and a final. The final was won

The 1955 Weymouth Scorchers.

by former Wembley rider Buster Brown and the meeting attracted a crowd of 2,000. A similar number of fans turned up the following week for a best pairs event won by Neath's Jon Erskine and Ron Harris.

On 3 August the Weymouth team reappeared under a new nickname, the Royals, and suitably a crown replaced the sun on their race jackets. The side included Buster Brown, Lew Coffin, Ken Vale and Bob Hughes, but the opening match, a challenge against the Rye House Red Devils, fell victim to bad weather, and thus became the first meeting ever to be rained off at Weymouth. Fortunately conditions improved the following week when the Royals recorded their first win. Brown led from the front scoring a 15-point maximum as Weymouth beat a Midlands Select 55-35. Rye House returned to Dorset on 17 August and snatched a 48-42 victory.

Provincial League champions Poole Pirates demonstrated their superiority when they travelled along the Dorset coast the following week, and won 51-39 with Geoff Mudge and Ross Gilbertson both unbeaten. Weymouth regained winning ways when they recorded a solid 55-29 win over a London Select in their penultimate home match.

The Scorchers completed their home fixtures at Radipole Lane with a massive 61-20 victory over a team misleadingly called the All Stars. Skipper Buster Brown and Pat Flanagan both scored 12-point maximums while the top visitor was Eric Eadon with 6. A visit to Rye House rounded off the season where the Red Devils repeated their earlier victory over the Scorchers.

Thirteen meetings would be staged at the Wessex Stadium in 1963 and the season opened on Whit Monday, 3 June, with not surprisingly the Whit Trophy, which was won by Frank Bettis. Jim Heard won all his qualifying heats and semi-final, but lost out in the final to Bettis, who had only finished third in his first race.

Buster Brown did not return to Weymouth so Lew Coffin took over the captaincy of the Royals. The Weymouth line-up included Ken Vale, former Plymouth Devils Ray Wickett and Lew Philp, John McGill and B. Billman. They beat Eastbourne 47-31 in their opening match on Friday 14 June, with Bob Hughes and Wickett joint top scorers with 11 points.

Eastbourne's Frank Bettis appeared for the Royals a week later scoring 10 points as they drew 39-39 with New Cross 'B'. A Best Pairs championship, scheduled for 28 June, was cancelled when continual rain waterlogged the track.

Weymouth's next home match was against a strong London Select which attracted a larger than average crowd. The visitors took an early lead but the Royals quickly levelled the scores before going six points ahead. However the visitors were managed by Poole team boss Ron Hart who used some shrewd tactics to overcome the deficit and allow the Londoners to go into the final heat holding a 2-point advantage. When the tapes rose Lew Philp and Pete Smith grabbed an early lead when both the visiting riders, Colin McKee and Terry Stone, missed the start, but they quickly recovered, passing Smith with one lap to go, then overtaking Philp on the final bend to win 42-36.

The Royals returned to winning ways on 12 July with victory over Exeter 'B'. Ken Vale scored his first 12-point maximum for Weymouth while the match also saw Exeter's legendary Goog Hoskin make a brief comeback, top-scoring for the Falcons with 8 points. Scrambles star Bryan 'Badger' Goss was also given a chance by Exeter, but failed to score. Royal's Frank Bettis notched just 3 points and announced his retirement due to business commitments.

The previously rained off Best Pairs meeting was restaged on 19 July and won by Ken Vale (14) and John McGill from Coffin and Hughes. Three old-time leg trailers, Phil Bishop, Mike Jenkins and Ray Cousins were among the competitors. Track announcer Robin Playsted recalls that veteran Phil Bishop, who was nicknamed the 'King of Crash', failed to tell his wife that he was taking part. Unfortunately Phil fell in the second heat and broke his ankle in two places – Mrs Bishop's reactions were not recorded!

A week later Weymouth were defeated 41-37 by their bogey team from the previous season, the Rye House Red Devils. Lew Coffin scored his first 12-point maximum and John McGill also enjoyed a good meeting even though he finished his last race holding the fuel tank in place.

Vale was the surprise winner of the Wessex Championship at the beginning of August. As Buster Brown was unable to defend his title the large crowd expected a straight fight between Provincial League stars Charlie Monk and Jon Erskine. Monk was unbeaten in his qualifying heats and semi-final, having defeated Vale in heat 6. The silent Australian, who refused to give interviews or pose for photographs, lined up in the final against Erskine, Pat Flanagan and Vale. For four glorious laps Monk and Vale fought neck and neck. First Monk dived under Vale only for the Weymouth rider to repeat the move on the next bend, but it was Vale who finally snatched victory by the narrowest of margins. Flanagan took third place.

Ray Wickett top scored with 11 points for the Royals in their next match, a 44-34 victory over the Midlands. The Royals claimed another victory on 16 August when they beat the Southern Stars 42-36 despite heavy rain before and during the match. The close-fought encounter started spectacularly when Tyburn Humphreys, later known as Tyburn Gallows, caught his handlebars in the fence and was flung across the track. Flanagan and Pete Munday tangled in heat 8 while John McGill following closely, laid his machine down to avoid further carnage. Lew Coffin top scored with 11 points as the Royals held on to a slender lead.

Hackney 'B' was the next Provincial League reserve team to visit Radipole Lane. The junior Hawks provided stiff opposition, storming away to win 45-32 with impressive teenager David Crane scoring a 12-point maximum in what proved to be an action-packed match. Five races had to be rerun and seven different riders fell. Hawks' Alan Jackman was taken to hospital with a suspected broken leg but later discharged with severe bruising. Ken Vale was the Royals' top scorer but a crucial factor in Weymouth's defeat was the form of skipper, Lew Coffin, who won his first race but failed to add to his score.

Weymouth visited Rye House on 25 August and although the Royals started well and even briefly went ahead, the Red Devils held off the Weymouth challenge to win 45-33. This was the Royals' last appearance of 1963 and the season closed with two junior matches, the Dorset Derby in which the East beat the South 42-36 and the Supporters Trophy run over twelve heats. The Dorset Derby involved riders from both Weymouth and Poole with Geoff Mudge topping the East score chart with 11, while leading South scorer was Ross Gilbertson with 13. Sadly threatening skies kept the crowd to a minimum. The Supporters' Trophy was won by Eric Eadon, who beat Stuart Wallace in a run off after they both finished on 11 points. The Junior Championship was won by Norman Brown, but again promoter John Pilbad was disappointed by the meagre size of the crowd.

The ill-fated Metropolitan League for junior teams was launched in 1964. The League consisted of Weymouth, Rayleigh, Ipswich, Eastbourne and Exeter plus Newpool, a combined Poole and Newport team. Exeter planned to race their home fixtures at Radipole Lane and the Weymouth season opened with a match between the junior Falcons and Newpool on 31 May. It would be a short lived arrangement and Exeter lost their only match 42-30.

Weymouth narrowly lost their first away match at Newport 36-35 on 19 June and two days later were defeated at Ipswich where new signing John Poyser and Ken Vale scored 10 points each. At Ipswich Pilbad found himself on other side of the camera when Anglia TV interviewed him prior to the racing. The Scorchers' only home Metropolitan match took place on 28 June when they beat Newpool 39-33. Poyser was missing because his wife was ill with pneumonia, and Vale dropped his only point to Pete Smith.

With Exeter having withdrawn after just one match, the Metropolitan League was showing ominous signs of falling apart. After a month's break the August bank holiday weekend saw Weymouth ride away at Rayleigh in their final League match on Saturday 1 August. It was poor show by the Scorchers as they were again without Poyser and Hughes, and although veteran Wal Morton and Malcolm Brown came in as replacements the Rockets won comfortably 49-23.

Two days later the season came to an abrupt end as disappointing crowd figures forced the promotion to abandon its last two scheduled meetings. The final meeting was the International All Stars Trophy, won by Exeter skipper Jimmy Squibb with a faultless 15-point maximum.

At the start of 1965 John Pilblad handed over the promotion to local enthusiast George Bargery in order to concentrate on his other interests at Ipswich. Sadly Bargery only managed to stage one ill-fated meeting, the Wessex Championship, on 13 April. Reports indicate that fewer than 100 fans turned up to see the title won by Pete Swain with a 15-point maximum. The line-up was drawn in the main from youngsters who attended Lew Coffin's training school. Lew himself took part but finished well down the order with 8 points, due to a serious hand injury sustained a few weeks earlier in a training session.

In fact one more meeting did take place, albeit unofficially. The 'meeting that never was' had been scheduled for 27 April as the Novice Best Pairs. For various reasons including a lack of paying customers the meeting was called off, but as all the programmed riders were already in the stadium, it was decided to run it as a practice session. Doug Dearden and John McGill were the winners. The first race saw Graham Locke fall and bring down Glen Tivey. In the rerun Edward Parker retired while John Hector fell off and was unable to restart. Consequently there were no finishers. Hector later became the track curator at Poole.

Thus Weymouth closed for a second time and the track was again given over to regular training schools run by Lew Coffin and Jimmy Squibb.

League racing returned to Radipole Lane in 1968 when Exeter promoters Wally Mawdsley and Pete Lansdale launched Weymouth in the newly founded British League Division Two. As they also planned to run Plymouth in the new League, former Falcon Howdy Byford was installed as manager. Howdy lived on site in a prefabricated building, which also doubled up as speedway office and riders' changing rooms.

The team was renamed the Eagles and assembled around Coventry loanee Tony Lomas, Poole junior Mike Vernam, and colourful Barry Duke. Home meetings would take place on Sunday afternoons to save the cost of replacing the derelict floodlights. This in itself was a brave move as at the time the Lord's Day Observance Society was still an extremely powerful organisation. Had the Eagles enjoyed a successful season it is possible that they may have paved the way for all Second Division teams to operate at the weekend. As it was the new Weymouth management quickly discovered that on sunny days the holidaymakers preferred the beach while on wet afternoons the cinema and bingo hall proved a stronger attraction.

The Eagles made their debut at Rayleigh, scene of the Scorchers' last match in 1955. Sadly it was not a dream start as Lomas and Carter failed to arrive after their car blew its big end en route down the M1 and without them the Eagles lost 47-31. In a bid to find replacements a phone call to West Ham resulted in the arrival of the Hammers' second-halfer Chris Yeatman, who promptly scored 12 points and earned himself a contract for the rest of the season.

Bad weather forced the postponement of the Eagles' opening match against Plymouth at the Wessex Stadium in late May. Loss of that meeting was a major blow, as early indications pointed to big attendance, and even the ACU referee George Allan's arrival at the stadium was delayed by the crowds.

Speedway eventually returned to Weymouth a week later when the Eagles defeated Plymouth 42-36. Middlesbrough were beaten but then both Crayford and Reading drew at Radipole Lane. Duke and Lomas both scored maximums in the home victory over Nelson Admirals. The next home match, against Rayleigh, was rained off and the following week's fixture against top of the League Belle Vue Colts looked set to suffer a similar fate. The match eventually went ahead despite dreadful conditions and the Colts quickly powered into an 18-6 lead after just four races. Although Lomas scored a 15-point maximum and Duke notched a couple of wins, Belle Vue won 43-34. Rayleigh returned the following week and after a close-run match led going into the final race. The Eagles needed a 5-1 for victory, and although the Weymouth duo of Lomas and Vernam led from the tapes, the latter fell on the last lap and Rayleigh won 40-38.

Rain-offs, poor results and falling attendances made for severe financial losses and put the future of the Eagles in serious doubt. The season was expected to end prematurely with a National League fixture against Canterbury. The promoters intended to complete their away fixtures against sides that had already visited the Wessex Stadium and then withdraw from the League. But after beating the Crusaders 48-29 it was agreed that the Eagles would race both fixtures against Berwick. The away match at Shielfield Park was brought forward by 24 hours to allow both teams extra time to travel to Dorset for the return leg. The Eagles lost 43-33 in the Borders but won 48-28 at home. This left the Bandits at the bottom of the table with Weymouth one slot above.

Kelvin Mullarkey.

Three away matches remained. The Eagles, still without an away win to their name, failed to break their duck; they went down 41-34 at Crayford, 63-15 at Belle Vue and 42-35 in a challenge match at Canterbury. The 63-15 massacre in Manchester saw the Eagles narrowly avoid a whitewash as the Colts rattled up the biggest Second Division win of the season. Mawdsley and Lansdale had had enough and the Eagles were withdrawn from the League, having eventually finished bottom.

Other than Lew Coffin's regular training schools no further speedway took place at Weymouth until 1974 when King's Lynn and Boston supremo, Cyril Crane and Gordon Parkins took charge at the Wessex Stadium with Ted Holding as their front man.

The team now became the Wizards and their colours changed to purple and white. Improvements were made to the stadium; the safety fence was replaced with one from Oxford and a new 300ft grandstand built. New floodlights were also installed which allowed the Wizards to select Tuesday as their race night. The National League had increased dramatically since 1968 and Weymouth now faced a home season of twenty-four matches. Could local interest be sustained for that long?

Kelvin Mullarkey, Bob Hughes, Steve Lomas, Nigel Couzens, Geoff Swindells, Russell Foot, Clark and Glyn Facey, Brian Paddington and Mark Sawyer formed the new team. Sadly it would not be a successful return for the Wizards who again finished bottom of the table after winning only ten of their thirty-six matches. Those victories all came at home and the Wizards also lost 83-72, on aggregate, to Boston in the opening round of the Knockout Cup.

The season opened not surprisingly with a challenge match against the management's other team the Boston Barracudas on Tuesday 2 April. The Wizards got off to a good start beating Boston in a challenge followed by a win over Swedish tourists Karparna, the first continental team to visit the Wessex Stadium. The first League points were taken from Long Eaton with Bob Hughes and Clark Facey scoring paid maximums. Further success came against Berwick but Eastbourne completed the double over the Wizards and then Peterborough Panthers won at Radipole Lane at the end of May.

In a bid to increase attendances the management switched the Wizards' home matches to Saturday night. Birmingham were the first weekend visitors and stormed to a 52-26 challenge match win. The track record was broken several times and Brummies

Arthur Browning ended the evening as the new holder with a time of 71.0 seconds. A week later the Barrow Bombers won 41½-36½ when Couzens and Tom Owen provided Radipole Lane's first dead heat.

The Wizards finally ended their disastrous run with a home victory over Boston. Further home victories were recorded against Peterborough and Rye House before the management accepted that Saturday night speedway was not working. A return to Tuesday night racing saw the home defeats continue with the Teeside Tigers becoming the sixth team to win at the Wessex Stadium that summer. Boston's Carl Glover was the first winner of what would become a regular annual event, the Sinalco Trophy, with a 15-point maximum.

That elusive first away win continued to elude the Wizards and their chances of avoiding the Second Division wooden spoon now depended on beating fellow strugglers Sunderland Gladiators at the Wessex Stadium. The Gladiators, riding what proved to be their last away match, trailed by 11 points after seven heats, but fought back to reduce the deficit to just 3 points. Three drawn heats followed then Sunderland finished strongly with a 5-1, which gave them victory by the narrowest of margins, 39-38. Worse was to come when Birmingham visited Radipole Lane a week later and hammered the Wizards 50-28. Brummies' John Hart lowered the track record to 70.6 seconds and, along with team-mates George Major, Arthur Browning and Keith Anderson, was unbeaten by a Weymouth rider.

A couple of matches were staged on Thursdays but nothing seemed to attract the holidaymakers and Weymouth thankfully completed their home fixtures with a win over Scunthorpe. Although the Wizards had completed the season, there was little to show for it and not surprisingly Crane and his associates relinquished their promotional interest at Weymouth.

The 1975 season saw more changes. Stadium owner Harry Davis, father of future England international John, took over as promoter. Skipper Bob Hughes was appointed manager and Martin Yeates, Brian Woodward, Vic Harding, Chris Robins, Tony Freegard, Melvyn Soffe and Richard Owen, along with Geoff Swindells, the sole survivor from '74, made up the team. Sadly these changes were no more successful as the Wizards again finished at the bottom of the table although Yeates and Woodward would go on to become Weymouth stalwarts.

The season opened on Easter Monday with the Wessex Rosebowl individual event. Unfortunately the meeting was abandoned after sixteen heats due to the weather, when Martin Yeates, unbeaten on 12 points, was declared the winner.

The new-look Wizards began with home and away defeats against Canterbury but again beat Karparna. Weymouth staged its first World Championship qualifying round on 22 April which was won by Eastbourne's Paul Gauchet with a 15-point maximum. Away from home the season followed the same old script with defeats at Workington, Berwick and Eastbourne. These were offset by a big 50-28 home Knockout Cup win over Peterborough at Radipole Lane in which Yeates scored 12 points.

Newport won an inter-League four-team tournament at the Wessex Stadium with Wasps' Phil Crump scoring a maximum. The Wizards used John Davis as a guest and finished a creditable joint second with Poole ahead of Exeter. In the second leg of the

Knockout Cup tie at the East of England showground the Panthers gradually whittled away the Wizards' 22-point lead and eventually went ahead on aggregate only for Yeates and Couzens to stun the fans by scoring a 5-1 which gave Weymouth overall victory 79-77.

Crayford snatched a last-heat draw in the National League at the Wessex Stadium and a week later Eastbourne won 45-35. More away defeats followed at Stoke and Paisley, while the home losses began to pile up as the Potters completed the double 41-37. Worse was to follow when Coatbridge arrived with only five riders. The Weymouth management agreed to help out by loaning them Russell Foot and Frank Harvey, both of whom were not currently in the Wizards' line-up. The Scottish team had little trouble in winning 43-34.

The heavy away defeats continued at Peterborough and Boston and after fourteen matches the Wizards had mustered just one League point. This dismal run ended on 10 June when Weymouth beat Crewe to notch their first League victory of the summer. A second success was gained against Bradford, before Birmingham inflicted another defeat.

Ellesmere Port and Newcastle both achieved home and away League doubles over Weymouth while Workington's 48-30 victory at Radipole Lane was the Wizards' biggest home defeat. Vic Harding won the Seyco Trophy with a 15-point maximum while a West German touring side was crushed 58-20. Peterborough were defeated in the League but a week later Boston tore the Wizards apart 50-28 in a crushing display.

The Wizards managed to beat Bradford on aggregate in the Knockout Cup and qualify for the semi-final, but their semi at Eastbourne was rained off and rearranged for a fortnight later. Unfortunately this was changed at short notice and added on to a three-match northern tour. The tour, not surprisingly, produced three more defeats, including a 61-15 hammering at Bradford, and at Arlington the tired Wizards were thrashed 60-18. Although Weymouth regained a modicum of respect by winning the second leg 42-36 it was the Eagles who qualified for the final.

The penultimate home match saw the Berwick Bandits pull back the Wizards' early 12-point lead to secure a draw. In the opening race Martin Yeates became the first Weymouth rider to break the Wessex Stadium track record with a time of 70.0 seconds. Weymouth completed their longest-ever season on 7 October with a 50-28 victory over Mildenhall. Sadly it did not save the Wizards from a second successive wooden spoon.

For 1976, his second season in charge, promoter Harry Davis rejected the temptation to boost his struggling team with experienced 'old hands' from the British League preferring instead to stick with his blossoming if youthful spearhead of Martin Yeates, Vic Harding and Chris Robins supported by graduates from the popular Weymouth training school. Geoff Mudge and Chris Julian were rumoured to be joining the Wildcats but never appeared, while Tim Bungay rode in the opening individual meeting but was not seen again.

The season opened on March 30 with the traditional big win over a Swedish touring side, this time Vetlanda. The Weymouth World Championship round on 13 April was won by Tony Featherstone with a 15-point maximum.

The Wizards' interest in the Knockout Cup was brief as they went out to Oxford in the preliminary round, but the League began with wins over Boston and Paisley. The

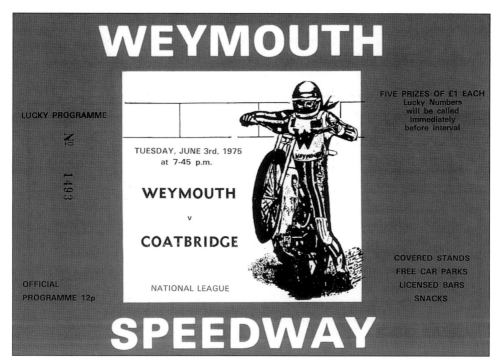

A 1975 programme cover.

Boston match saw Gerald 'Jaffa' Purkiss make his Weymouth debut on loan from Exeter. The usual pattern was already set with the Wizards winning at home and losing away. Scunthorpe arrived in Dorset several riders short and were hammered 50-28. Despite the score line there no lack of drama and most of it revolved around the Saints' hard riding Colin Cook. Later that week, on Thursday 3 June, Weymouth created club history at Stoke when they finally won an away match. Having trailed in the early stages the Wizards put together a run of 4-2s before Martin Yeates and Gerald Purkiss took maximum points in the final race to win 41-37. Yeates' win completed a 15-point maximum.

Life returned to normal 24 hours later at Workington where Weymouth lost 55-22. There was no triumphant homecoming either as Stoke were the visitors and gained full revenge by winning 41-37. Just to prove that away win was no fluke the Wizards went to Scunthorpe and drew 39-39 but lost by a single point in a later revenge challenge match at Stoke. June had also seen Australian Danny Kennedy join Weymouth on loan from Newport. Another addition was promising young Londoner, Billy Spiers, who replaced Purkiss, who had been injured.

The Seyco Soft Drinks Trophy at the beginning of August was won by Stoke skipper Les Collins. Meanwhile the Wizards suffered a run of injuries. Without Vic Harding they lost at home to Ellesmere Port. Further defeats by Canterbury, Newcastle and Rye House followed. The visit of the Rockets was a particularly bad night for Weymouth as Jack Walker broke his leg while laying his machine down to avoid the fallen Rob Cooper in the first race. Four heats later Rockets' Ted Hubbard brought down Kennedy as a result of which the young Australian broke a bone in his hand, which kept him out for the rest of the season. In the second half Harding fell and hurt his arm. Robins was already on the injured list having been hurt in a previous match. Weymouth managed to finish with a win over Workington thanks mainly to Spiers who scored a career best 13 points. After twice gracing the bottom of the League the Wizards now had the satisfaction of finishing above three other teams.

The winter saw big changes at Weymouth. Martin Yeates was transferred to Oxford, and Billy Spiers moved to King's Lynn. Into their places came Geoff Swindells, persuaded out of retirement, and Mal Corradine who had ridden for both Cradley and Oxford in 1976. Danny Kennedy, Vic Harding and Chris Robins would spearhead the team along with Gerald Purkiss, who had been purchased from Exeter for £300. But due to a wrangle over personal terms Purkiss did not appear until June and then only rode in three matches before retiring. The early season saw Roger Stratton, Ricky Owen and Dick Partridge complete the line-up.

The 1977 season began early for Weymouth with an away challenge match at Oxford. Yeates scored a paid maximum against his former team mates as the Cheetahs won 48-30. The League proper got off to an equally early start with away defeats at Newcastle and Ellesmere Port at the end of March.

The Wizards' home season opened on Tuesday 5 April with a challenge match victory over Newport Dragons. Two days later the Wizards completed the double at Somerton Park. Sadly Weymouth's encouraging start came to an abrupt halt when the Mildenhall Fen Tigers visited Radipole Lane for the first National League match and won 40-38 on 24 April. Partridge was dropped to make way for Mal Corradine who made his Weymouth debut.

The Wizards had made a quick exit from the Knockout Cup going out to Boston by a single point on aggregate. Rumours had circulated for some time that Robins wanted a move, and he duly departed for Leicester. He was rapidly replaced by a 16-year-old novice, Sean Willmott. Willmott was the protégé of training school supremo Lew Coffin and took regular interval rides at a number of tracks. He had promised that when he became sixteen he would sign for Weymouth but as his birthday approached several other tracks made him impressive offers. However Sean was as good as his word and joined the Wizards making his debut at Newport in the same match as Robins made his exit.

On 19 July Vic Harding also made his last appearance for Weymouth in a draw against Newcastle before transferring to Hackney. Two years later the popular Londoner lost his life in a track crash at Waterden Road. Harding was replaced at Weymouth by Bristol-based grass tracker, Richards Evans who later became promoter at Swindon.

The Wizards were once again struggling, having gained just 15 League points from twenty-five matches. Even Stoke, who were vying with Weymouth for the wooden spoon slot, won at the Wessex Stadium. In August Harry Davis made two further additions to his side. He signed former Wimbledon junior Rob Jones, and also talked Cornishman Chris Julian into making a comeback. Neither proved to be a consistent scorer but their presence turned the tables, and the Wizards even managed to win away at Workington. Weymouth were not completely out of the woods as Glasgow still achieved a win at Radipole Lane, but the Wizards eventually managed to finish seventeenth from twenty in the League table. Kennedy represented Weymouth in the National League Riders Championship, finishing a lowly thirteenth with 4 points. The Wizards' season closed with an inter-League challenge against Poole which the Pirates won 41-37.

At the end of the season Davis revealed that he was looking for someone to take over Weymouth Speedway. Not long after Christmas Hackney promoter Len Silver reached an agreement with Davis and announced that he and his Hawks team manager Dave Erskine would run the track in 1978. Silver was soon making extensive improvements to the stadium's facilities. He gave the team their fifth new nickname, the Wildcats, and began to rebuild the line-up. Danny Kennedy became a fully fledged Weymouth rider, Malcolm Corradine came back along with Geoff Swindells and Sean Willmott while Canadian Gary Ford was signed on loan from Poole as a replacement for retired Chris Julian. Richard Evans only lasted three matches before being replaced by Malcolm Shakespeare. An Australian, Mick Conroy, was brought in as a replacement for Rob Jones who had decided to stay at home in Melbourne.

The first three home matches saw the Wildcats exceed the 50-point mark with wins over Barrow, Boston and Scunthorpe, but an international challenge match against Red Star Prague was lost to heavy rain. The big wins were interspersed by away defeats at Peterborough, Oxford and Eastbourne. The Eagles also shattered Weymouth's unbeaten home record with a 50-28 win at Radipole Lane on 23 May.

Peterborough, Stoke, Newcastle, and Canterbury also won at the Wessex Stadium. Canterbury were victorious twice as the Crusaders also achieved the double in the first round of the Knockout Cup. Weymouth started winning again when Edinburgh came south in July and from then on successfully completed their home fixtures, even beating their Dorset neighbours Poole Pirates in a challenge match in September. The Wildcats also recorded away wins at Scunthorpe, where Kennedy scored a maximum, and Teesside.

Sadly crowds failed to meet expectations, with the exception of an inter-League fours tournament involving Bristol, Exeter and Poole which produced a record attendance. Bristol, were the eventual winners and Bulldogs' Steve Gresham set a new track record, 68.12 seconds in heat 2. It did not stand for long as fellow American Scott Autrey of Exeter broke it in the very next race, with a time of 68.0 seconds. Kennedy again represented the Wildcats in the National League Riders Championship but fell in his first race and finished with eight points.

The year 1979 saw a further change of promotion when Reading's Brian Constable took over from Silver and Erskine. It was to prove another season of falling gates and disappointment. Brian Woodward, Doug Underwood and Bob Coles formed the spearhead and were supported by Mal Shakespeare, Terry Tulloch, Garry May, Ken Bowen, Barry Allaway, Nigel Davis, Mark DeKok, Derek Hole and Greg Joynt.

The season started badly with a home defeat by Oxford in a challenge match. The Wildcats also lost away at Canterbury in their opening National League fixture before Czech touring side Red Star Prague arrived at Wessex Stadium and hammered the

Chris Robins.

Wildcats 52-26. A second international defeat followed a week later when Swedish League outfit Getingarna won 40½-37½.

Weymouth also lost to Rye house in the Knockout Cup and finished bottom of their Fours qualifying group. League points also proved hard to come by with home defeats by Ellesmere Port and Peterborough interspersed with a draw against Oxford. A victory was achieved over Nottingham Outlaws before Middlesbrough inflicted another defeat at the start of July. Exeter won an inter-League four-team event which also included Poole and Reading while Edinburgh's George Hunter was the winner of the Seyco Trophy.

The season came to a dismal conclusion during September starting with Rye House inflicting the Wildcats' the worst defeat of the year, a 60-18 thrashing at Hoddesdon. Canterbury's victory at the Wessex Stadium was followed by a 56-22 mauling by Ellesmere Port. Malcolm Shakespeare was forced to drop out with a continuing knee injury and League champions elect Rye House returned to Dorset and won for the second time, 52-26.

Mildenhall, destined to finished runners-up to the Rockets, inflicted another heavy defeat a week later, but the Wildcats managed to end the League campaign on a winning note by beating Scunthorpe 46-32. An inter-League challenge match against Exeter brought down the curtain on another forgettable season with the Wildcats failing to match the top Falcons who won 44-34.

The Wildcats finished seventeenth of twenty and, perhaps not surprisingly, Brian Constable pulled out leaving Weymouth's future in considerable doubt. But team manager Phil Lock refused to allow the Wildcats to die. He strove to find a new promoter and eventually succeeded in persuading local property developer and millionaire businessman Mervyn Stewkesbury to take over the doomed club. Stewkesbury knew nothing about speedway but learned quickly and was not afraid to spend money on building a successful team. In fact his readiness to pay big money did not always endear him to his fellow promoters.

He stunned the speedway world by bringing former Belle Vue Aces star Chris Pusey out of retirement to join Woodward and Coles, and also forked out a reputed £8,000 to make Martin Yeates a permanent Weymouth asset. Another returnee was Mal Corradine, re-signed from Middlesbrough for £2,500.

Tipped by many as likely champions the Wizards started 1980 by winning a four team tournament at Exeter. Success continued at home the following evening when the Wildcats' opened their home season with victory over Oxford in a challenge match in which Simon Wigg made his debut. Wigg, on loan from Reading, failed to score but that would soon change.

On May bank holiday the Wildcats lost 40-38 in a last heat decider at Exeter after Bob Coles was controversially excluded in a first-bend incident. The next night Weymouth exacted full revenge by beating the Falcons 48-30, but lost Coles with a broken leg. Two weeks later Pusey achieved his best and only double-figure score of the season, 10 paid 11, at Glasgow where the Wildcats lost narrowly 40-38. Coles amazingly returned against the Rye House at the beginning of July. The following week Oxford's John Hack won the Seyco Trophy.

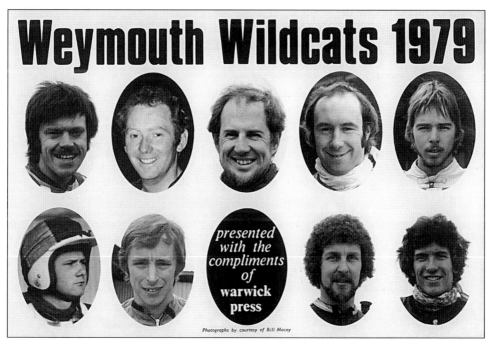

The 1979 Weymouth Wildcats.

September saw the Wildcats achieve a rare away win against the struggling Workington and the promising second-halfer Steve Schofield made his team debut away at Boston.

Yeates had justified his National League record transfer fee with seven full maximums and although Wigg missed half of Weymouth's away fixtures due to his continental grass and long-track commitments his efforts more than made up for the disappointing form shown by Pusey and Carradine. Doubtless Lew Coffin's influence had played a major role in signing Wigg and Schofield but in spite of showing so much promise Weymouth finished well down the table in seventeenth place. But far more disappointing was the continued lack of public support.

Weymouth finally achieved success in 1981. With Pusey and Corradine axed the Wildcats line-up consisted of Martin Yeates, Simon Wigg, Brian Woodward and Bob Coles. Malcolm Shakespeare had returned from injury while the reserves were Terry Tulloch and Mark Dekok. Waiting in the wings were Kevin Young, back after a spell in the German League, and grass tracker Steve Schofield. Another important addition was that of experienced Australian rider and engineer Neil Street as team manager.

The National League campaign began superbly with away wins at Scunthorpe and Wolverhampton. Poole's Neil Middleditch won the World Championship qualifying round at Wessex Stadium on 7 April with 14 points. Middleditch dropped his only point to Yeates in the first heat when the Weymouth rider broke the track record with a time of 66.4 seconds.

Wolverhampton marked their first appearance in Dorset by forcing a 39-39 draw in the opening home League match. Wildcats' boss Mervyn Stewkesbury promptly purchased Les Rumsey, then one of the National League's top scorers and the Wolves' skipper, in a deal which also brought Steve Crockett to Radipole Lane. Rumsey made his debut for Weymouth at Boston, where he scored 3 points as the Wildcats went down 51-27. Coles failed to score in that match and was dropped. He continued for a couple of weeks in the second half before going on loan to Exeter. Crockett also made a point-less first appearance at Boston.

Rumsey quickly found his form, scoring 9, 12 and 11 in the next three matches, as the Wizards launched a run of five successive victories. The flow was halted at Middlesbrough but resumed at Ellesmere Port on Friday 31 July where Weymouth won 41-37 with Rumsey scoring 14 paid 15. After losing 43-35 at Exeter, revenge was gained the following night at Wessex Stadium where the Wildcats launched an impressive winning streak which peaked in August with eight successive victories home and away. With the exception of a 45-33 loss at Peterborough on 4 September Weymouth would have remained unbeaten to the end of the season. This amazing run carried them into second place in the League table behind champions Middlesbrough.

The Wildcats' League success was not repeated in the Knockout Cup where after a first round bye and home and away wins over Workington, Weymouth lost to Berwick. Martin Yeates topped the Wildcats averages with a splendid 10.20 and also briefly held the Silver Helmet after beating holder Dave Perks from Oxford before losing it to Glasgow's Steve Lawson.

The new 50-point rule was introduced in 1982. The Wildcats were over the limit and forced to shed points. Malcolm Shakespeare retired and long serving Brian Woodward

WEYMOUTH
Speedway

Tuesday 2 October
at 7.45 p.m.
WEYMOUTH
v
EXETER
Inter-League Challenge

OFFICIAL PROGRAMME 15p

A 1979 programme cover.

Bob Coles crashes out as Martin Yeates attempts to split Exeter's Rob Maxfield and John Barker.

was released to comply with the regulations thus becoming possibly the first rider to lose his team place due to the points limit. Weymouth managed to hold on to Simon Wigg despite his demands for a transfer and the efforts of several British League teams to lure him away. With Wigg the Wildcats had a very powerful look about them, as Martin Yeates, Les Rumsey, and Steve Schofield had all been retained along with Steve Crockett and Terry Tulloch. A new addition was Australian Stan Bear.

The new season began with the traditional challenge matches against Oxford. The Wildcats lost by four points at Cowley but won the home leg convincingly 56-40. Easter Monday saw Weymouth lose another challenge at Exeter, but Simon Wigg won the World Championship qualifier at Wessex Stadium. The Wildcats, minus Wigg, lost their opening League match at Boston by 20 points but quickly gained revenge by beating the Barracudas in Dorset and the following weekend collected their first away points with a 55-41 victory at Scunthorpe.

Tulloch quit and returned to Australia. He was replaced by Rob Mather, who was unable to make his scheduled debut at Canterbury in the first round of the Knockout Cup due to a bout of flu. The Wildcats lost at Kingsmead but stormed through to the next round thanks to a big win in the home leg. In the next round Weymouth drew at Peterborough and then won at home to earn a semi-final place against Newcastle. Weymouth went down 63-32 in the first leg at Brough Park and had to use rider replacement for the now injured Les Rumsey in the return at Wessex Stadium. The clash with the Diamonds was the second home match of the week, Mildenhall having been the visitors on the Tuesday, and went ahead despite a torrential downpour an hour before the start. The Wildcats' fight-back collapsed midway through the meeting and although

Wigg managed to spoil Joe Owen's maximum, the Diamonds stormed to a 61-35 victory, 124-67 on aggregate. Shortly afterwards Rumsey, who had failed to maintain his form of the previous season, went on loan to Canterbury.

Newcastle, having won at Weymouth in the National League during June, returned the following week for a revenge challenge match and this time the Wildcats won 57-39. Colourful Australian John McNeill had been signed from Cradley earlier in the season but did not make his Weymouth debut until later in the season. August began with victory over British League Swindon in a challenge match and the Wildcats' hopes of catching the League leaders were boosted when they achieved a big away win at Peterborough. Wigg and Schofield both scored paid maximums and Wigg also broke the track record.

The Wildcats' three-match northern tour began at Middlesbrough where Simon Wigg made National League history by scoring a 21-point maximum. The next night at Edinburgh Wiggy again took seven rides but had to be content with 17 points. Wigg was missing for the final match at Berwick due to a continental booking so this time it was Steve Schofield's turn to score an 18-point maximum as Weymouth snatched a narrow 49-47 victory.

With the end of the season fast approaching, Wigg was circulated as being available for transfer to the British League during the winter. Simon had been given permission to miss Weymouth's home match with Peterborough to prepare for the following weekend's world long-track final, which also prevented him representing the Wildcats in the National League Riders championship at Wimbledon. Yeates scored a 15-point maximum against the Panthers but only managed eleventh place at Wimbledon.

The Wildcats' home season ended with a win over Long Eaton and a week later a meagre crowd saw Rob Mather declared the winner of the Stars of Tomorrow Trophy after winning all his races before torrential rain forced the meeting to be abandoned. Weymouth completed their League fixtures on a winning note at Oxford where Simon Wigg bid farewell to the National League with a 15-point maximum.

Wigg eventually joined Cradley, and was replaced by Oxford's Simon Cross. McNeil, Crockett and Mark Minnett also left Weymouth that winter. The Wildcats went into 1983 with a line-up which still included Yeates, Bear and Schofield plus Cross, Ian Humphreys, a new Australian Chris Martin and 16-year-old newcomer David Biles.

During the winter the promoting company was restructured. Former supporters' club officials Alan Hodder and Pete Ansell joined Richard Loder and Brian Pierce as directors. Later in the year they would become co-promoters and take over the day-to-day running of the speedway with Ansell acting as general manager, and Hodder race night presenter.

The Weymouth season began with a home win over Crayford. A week later the World Championship qualifying round was won by Poole's Kevin Smith, while the Wildcats scored their first away win at Peterborough on 15 April. Further success followed with home and away wins over Boston in the first round of the Knockout Cup. April ended with a 48-47 home victory over Glasgow during which unfortunately Gordon Humphreys broke his arm.

May saw the Wildcats suffer their only home League defeat when Milton Keynes won 50-44. Another home point was dropped when Mildenhall drew 48-48 at the start of

June while Newcastle also forced a draw later in the season. Weymouth went on to win four more away National League matches, at Oxford, Glasgow, Stoke and Long Eaton, before eventually finishing in fourth place.

Martin Yeates and Simon Cross won the National Pairs championship at Belle Vue. It was the first time that a club had won the competition in successive years, Yeates having won with Simon Wigg at Swindon the previous year. In June the Wildcats won at Glasgow in the Knockout Cup. Already facing a glut of fixtures, the management now had to find a date for the home leg.

Weymouth were grouped with Canterbury, Milton Keynes and Exeter in their qualifying group of the National Fours with matches on four successive days. After 63 races the Wildcats faced a last-heat decider with Canterbury for the second qualifying place. Yeates duly beat the Crusaders' skipper Denzil Kent to ensure the Wildcats of a place at Peterborough on finals day, where sadly Weymouth finished last in their semi-final group.

Having overcome Glasgow in the Knockout Cup the Wildcats again met Newcastle Diamonds in the semi-final. To avoid an unnecessary delay the Diamonds agreed to switch their League fixture at Radipole Lane in early August to a cup match, which the Wildcats won 55-41. August also saw Weymouth suffer a spate of injuries. Rob Mather broke his leg at Long Eaton, Schofield fractured a collarbone in the next home match, then Ian Humphreys his wrist and David Biles a bone in a foot.

Tuesday 16 August saw the mighty Cradley Heath Heathens, complete with Simon Wigg, visit Dorset for the now annual British League challenge match. The BSPA refused Weymouth permission to use Phil Crump as a guest, but although the Wildcats included Exeter's Rob Ashton the Heathens won 62-34.

Schofield returned within the month, scoring a 15-point maximum against Long Eaton. The following Monday the second leg of the Knockout Cup semi-final took place at Newcastle. Although Weymouth lost 54-42 on the night they won 89-85 on aggregate and would meet Exeter in the final.

On Saturday 24 September Martin Yeates finished third in the National League Riders Championship at Wimbledon. The first leg of the Knockout Cup Final took place at Exeter on Monday 10 October where the Falcons quickly gained a 17-point lead. But by the end the Wildcats had reduced Exeter's advantage to a mere 9 points. A delighted Mervyn Stewkesbury told the local press: 'The Cup is ours!'

The next evening the Wildcats were equally confident as Yeates and Gordon Humphreys opened the proceedings with a 5-1. But the Falcons retaliated with a maximum of their own courtesy of former Wildcat Bob Coles and Kevin Price. Although Weymouth continued to whittle away at Exeter's advantage, the Falcons never gave up and at the end, despite the Wildcats winning 52-44, Exeter won the Cup by a single point, 96-95.

Stewkesbury later announced that Weymouth had continued to lose money, £10,000 in 1983, but he had virtually agreed a new 5-year lease with landlord John Davis which would give him sole rights within the stadium, including the training schools. Early in 1984 the Wildcats future was again threatened by the collapse of the management's highly successful fundraising lottery scheme. Weymouth's hopes of achieving further on track success were also dented by the departure to the British League of Simon Cross, Steve Schofield, and Stan Bear. While these moves deprived the Wildcats of their top riders the resulting transfer fees effectively kept Weymouth in business. A further blow to their hopes of success came with the news that Martin Yeates had been transferred to Swindon for a reputed £6,000 fee.

In just a few weeks the Wildcats' line-up had been decimated, but help came from an unexpected quarter. Exeter had returned to the British League and as a result Weymouth were able to sign ex-Falcons Alun Rossiter and John Barker, who even brought his former Eastbourne team mate Colin Ackroyd with him. Later Exeter juniors, Kevin Price, Michael Coles, and Mike Semmonds would also join the Wildcats.

The season opened in April with the South Dorset Triangle, which enabled team manager Neil Street to see all his riders in action against each other.

The Wildcats made an encouraging start with an away draw at Canterbury in the Knockout Cup. Ackroyd aggravated an old knee injury and was not seen again. In the return at Radipole Lane the Crusaders rapidly turned the tables to win 44-34. A second home defeat followed on Easter Monday when the Hackney Kestrels won the National League opener. This match was to prove a watershed in the career of David Biles. Rated as a 2-point man in 1983, Biles showed real potential by scoring 11 against the Kestrels.

Weymouth's first wins came in mid May against Peterborough and newcomers Arena Essex. Gordon Humphreys was suspended after failing to arrive on two occasions and shortly afterwards his brother Ian joined Arena Essex, they were replaced by Price and Coles.

The loss of the '83 heat leaders was soon being felt at the turnstiles while the casualty list was also growing. Rob Mather broke a bone in his hand at Scunthorpe, and never regained his team place, while Kiwi Chris Martin dropped out after five matches. After a heavy defeat at Canterbury, Weymouth's fortunes were unexpectedly boosted by the arrival of American Shawn McConnell at Swindon. McConnell went straight into the Robins' line-up at the expense of Martin Yeates, who in turn was persuaded to rejoin Weymouth. The impact of his return was instantaneous. Boston were defeated at Radipole Lane

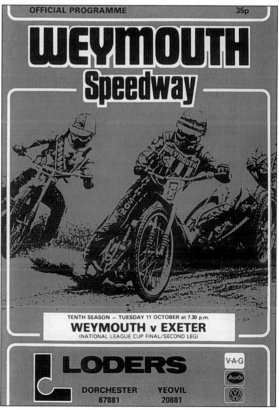

A 1983 programme cover.

and the reinforced Wildcats scored home and away wins over Edinburgh. Success was short-lived as the following night Weymouth crashed 51-27 at Berwick and Rossiter broke his collarbone.

Yeates, keen to prove Swindon wrong, became the first English National League rider to reach the Overseas Final of the World Championship, regained his 10-plus average and along with Rossiter finished third in the National League Pairs at Hackney. Sadly there was little success for the Wildcats as a team and they dropped to thirteenth in the League table.

An all-star four team tournament involving the Wildcats, Exeter, Swindon and Oxford at Wessex Stadium was abandoned – due to a rain-soaked track – before the opening heat could be rerun and almost resulted in a riot when holidaymakers among the spectators demanded their money back. To add to the Weymouth management's difficulties the Rye House team walked out the following week complaining about the state of the track after a weekend banger meeting.

The Rye House match was eventually restaged on 11 September and sadly proved to be the last public speedway meeting ever staged at Radipole Lane. Throughout the summer rumours had circulated that the site was being sold off to a supermarket company. This uncertainty eventually forced the Weymouth management to switch their entire operation to Poole just weeks before the 1985 season was due to start.

A final training school match on 2 November 1985 saw Weymouth lose to Wimbledon. Although the proposed supermarket never materialised it was announced in 1986 that all motor sport would cease at the stadium, which was subsequently redeveloped at the cost of £1 million as a football ground.

Several different attempts have since been made to bring speedway back to Weymouth. At one time it looked as though Phil Lock would use a former banger track at Portland, then more recently former Poole junior Brian White announced that he intended to construct a Conference League track in a quarry also on Portland. This project was stillborn when it was discovered that the proposed track would be on a Site of Special Scientific Interest. An attempt by White to re-establish speedway at Radipole Lane also failed to materialise and as 2002 came to a close news broke that, undeterred, he had found another possible site at Chickerell on the outskirts of Weymouth.